# Bagnall
## School & Village
## Memories

The bus stranded in the snow at Light Oaks Reservoir.

# Anne Lewis

This book is dedicated to my grandson
Thomas Lewis Charles Foster

## ACKNOWLEDGEMENTS

Sincere thanks go to the following people and organisations, because without their help this book would not have been written.

| | | | |
|---|---|---|---|
| Stafford Archives | Sheila Tipper | Hanley Archives | Margaret Walley |
| Leek Library | Terry Chetwin | Brian Lewis | Kath Jury |
| Elizabeth Bass | Ron Beckett | Margaret Heath | Trevor Raistrick |
| Margaret Davies | Dorothy Welch | Pauline Raistrick | Denise Johnson |
| Audrey Rennie | Jim Bailey | Alan Beckett | Sheila Woodward |
| Millie Hilditch | Jan Crumpler | Rachel Cartwright | Margaret Ball |
| Elaine Wood | Betty Hughes | Valerie Whittaker | Kathleen Harper |
| Joyce Rowley | Freda Stubbs | Mary Wain | Betty Yorke |
| Gladys Croft | Mary Cairns | Daphne Evans | Victor Podmore |
| Madge Peat | John Bailey | John Sheldon | Josephine Sheldon |

*The photos on pps 10 & 11 are copies of fine watercolour paintings of Mr T.W. Mountford who has kindly given permission for me to use them. Mr Mountford is a member of the Society of Staffordshire Artists and exhibits widely in the area and at The Gallery in Leek.*

*This photo of the Hollies school on p. 43 is from Mrs Dorothy M. Norris's book The Hollies School published in 2004 and still available from local bookshops or direct from the author 01484 851976.*

**CHURNET VALLEY BOOKS**
1 King Street, Leek, Staffordshire. 01538 399033
www.leekbooks.co.uk
© Anne Lewis and Churnet Valley Books 2005
ISBN 1 904546 33 1

# CONTENTS

# FOREWORD

Bagnall School was burnt down thirty-six years ago and for some considerable time now I have felt that if some of the personal memories were not recorded in some way they would be lost for ever. To begin with this was my aim, and then as the work progressed it was suggested that more of the village history and other memories of events should be included too. So interwoven with the school memories are some of these events.

Anne Lewis
Spring 2005

Although this pedigree is much later, the Bagnall family were originally located around the village. Dr Plott (17th century) says they had a mansion in the township.

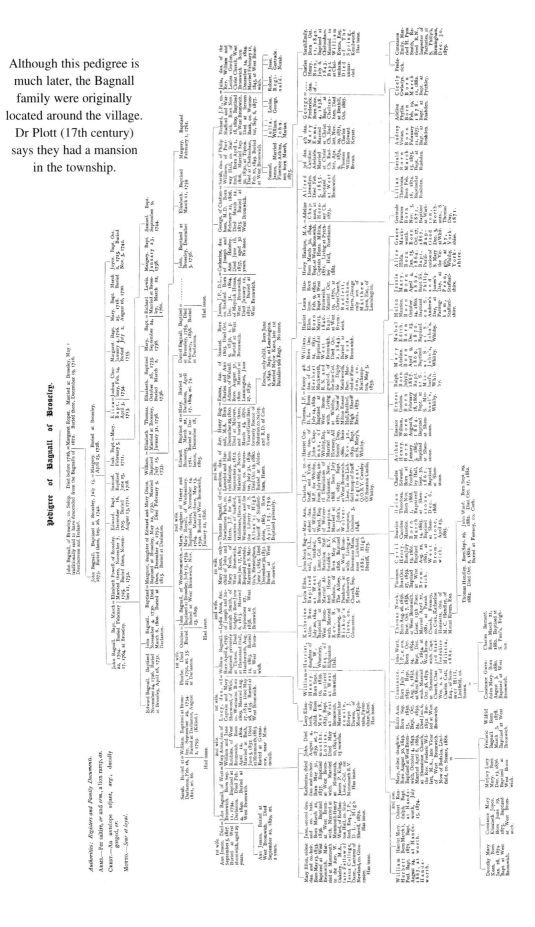

Pedigree of Bagnall of Broseley.

# Chapter 1
# Bagnall Village

Bagnall village has been formally known as Bagenholt, Badegenall, Baginholt and Bagenhall. It is a hilltop village 2 miles to the South of Endon and 6 miles North East of Newcastle, bounded by the parishes of Norton, Leek and Cheddleton. Its history can be traced back to Anglo Saxon times, when it was merely a clearing in a wild track of forest and scrub, although an axe head discovered at Moor Head Farm in 1964 would suggest that people were settled in this area more than 2,000 years ago. Bagnall itself is not mentioned in the Domesday Book of 1086 - it was possibly included in the manor of Endon.

When Henry I came to the throne in 1100 Bagnall was a crown possession. The king rewarded the barons for loyalty to the crown by granting them crown lands. William Pantulf, Baron of Wem in Shropshire, was given half of the extensive manor of Bagnall, to be held under Robert Earl of Shrewsbury.

After the death of William Pantulf, Bagnall was inherited by his son, Ivo Pantulf. He did not hold it for very long and it passed to Adam of Audley in exchange for the constablewick of Thak (Talke) at an annual rent of 12d. Adam of Audley acquired the two half manors of Bagnall and Stanley and adopted the name of Adam of Stanley.

The de Bagnall family took their name from the village. In 1204 Robert de Bagenhall and William de Bagenhall both held land in the village. Members of the family moved to Newcastle under Lyme and in the 1500s John Bagnall was the mayor of Newcastle five times. Honest Ralph Bagenhall was reputed to feature in Tennyson's *Queen Mary*.

In 1219 the Cistercian Abbey was founded by Robert de Audley at Abbey Hulton and was linked to Bagnall by the old roadway known locally as 'The Stumps' or 'The Monks' Way'. This was the route the monks took through Woodhead to Bagnall and beyond. Salt was also transported along this road. The packhorse mules travelled through the area, giving rise to such names as Salters Wells, Salters Brook and Salters Lane.

Some prominent features of the Bagnall area developed as the land was enclosed. The dry stone walls that were built around the fields and a number of quarries were established where the stone was extracted. The earliest buildings were the longhouses where the animals lived at one end of the building and the residents at the other. By 1563 there were ten households of note living in the Bagnall area.

The Jacobite rebellion had associations with Bagnall when in 1745 the young pretender to the throne, Prince Charles Edward Stuart (Bonnie Prince Charlie) passed through North Staffordshire on his way to Derby. He was at the head of his kilted army of Highlanders in his unsuccessful bid to establish the Stuart claim to the throne of England. William Murhall from Bagnall Hall captured one of the men who had strayed near to his home as he pillaged for food to feed the army. The poor man was believed to have been

BUCKNALL-CUM-BAGNALL, with the EAVES and UBBERLEY, form a *district rectory*, as noticed at page 222, though they maintain their poor jointly with the rest of the parish of Stoke-upon-Trent. They comprise about 4200 acres of land, extending from 1 to 4 miles E. and N.E. of Hanley, bounded by the Trent and the Cauldon canal. In 1841, they had 1608 inhabitants, of whom 638 were in Bucknall village, 1½ mile from Hanley; 374 in Bagnall; 382 in the Eaves, 3 miles E. of Hanley; and 214 in Ubberley. Sir George Chetwynd, Ralph Sneyd, Esq., and Miss Sparrow own a great part of the soil. BUCKNALL CHURCH, on the hill 1½ mile E. of Hanley, is a small edifice, which was rebuilt in 1718, and the living is a *rectory*, with Bagnall curacy annexed to it, valued at about £530 per annum, and in the patronage and incumbency of the Rev. Edward Powys, of Cheddleton. *Bagnall Chapel* is a small neat brick building, which was rebuilt in 1834, at the cost of £520, and stands on a bold hill, 4 miles N.E. of Hanley, in Totmonslow Hundred. In 1827, *Wm. Willet*, died at the Eaves, aged 105 years. *Bucknall School* was founded about 1719, when Wm. Shalcross left £5 a year for schooling 12 poor children. The New Connexion Methodists have a chapel at Bucknall, built in 1824. *In the following* DIRECTORY *those marked thus * reside in Bagnall*, and the others in *Bucknall, or where specified*.

Two directory extracts for
Bagnall.
Above, *White's Directory* 1851

Below, *The Potteries & Newcastle Directory* 1912

Allen Samuel, church clerk
Beardmore Jeremiah, maltster
Bentley Geo., *National schoolmaster*
Brookes Ralph, joiner & wheelwright
Brownsword Thos. ironfounder, &c
Chappell Geo. & Co., flint grinders
Forrister Robt. & Jno. coal masters, *Holly Greave;* h Bleakhill
Forrister Jas. clerk, BrassingtonFarm
Green Sarah, schoolmistress
Harp & Waine, coal masters, *Brownfields*
Harrison Wm. tailor
Hawley Jph. clerk, Wheatley Cottage
Knight John King & Son, *Ubberley Hall Colliery;* h Golden hill
Lees Abraham, wheelwright
Perrins Geo. agent ‖ Maer Mrs E.
Perry Hugh Booth, flint grinder
Perry Thos. ironmonger, at Hanley
Pierce Joseph, railway clerk
Ridgway John, *Ubberley Colliery;* house Cauldon place
Staley John, mine agt. *Ubberley*
Townsend & Plant, colliery owners
Townsend Rev Wm. M., B.A., curate
Wedgwood Abner, gent. *Eaves*

INNS AND TAVERNS.
Bowling-green, John Johnson
Dog and Partridge, Thos. Forrister
*King's Arms, Wm. Adams
Red Lion, Wm. Austin

BEERHOUSES.
Brownsword Sar.
Edwards Wm.
Hind Wm.
Holdcroft James
Jackson John
Willshaw George

BLACKSMITHS.
Brownsword Geo
Moreton John

BOOT & SHOE MKS.
Atkin Wm.
Holdcroft James
Ridge Wm.

BUTCHERS.
Rhead Sampson, (& flour dealr)
Sargeant George
Scragg Joseph
Woolliscroft Geo.

FARMERS.
Atkins Henry, *Ubberley*
*Basnett Daniel
Bayley Wm. *Bentilee*
Beardmore Jerh.
Brown Jph. *Eaves*
Colclough Ts. do
Dale Ralph, *Ubberley Hall*
Docksey John
Fletcher James
Forrister James
*Limer John
Martin John
*Myatt Enoch
*Salt John
*Steel Ephm.
Timms John, *Holly Greave*
Wolliscroft Saml.

BAGNALL PARISH COUNCIL.
T. M. Parry (chairman); F. Arden,
C. H Amos. E. W. Jackson, Thomas Edge
John Howarth
Clerk.—J. T. Yarwood.
Postal Address.-Bagnall, Stoke-on-Trent
Nearest Railway Station
- Stockton Brook N.S.R.
Overseers.
Charles Hry Amos, Enoch Wm Jackson
Area.—1,656 acres. Population.—563.

ALPHABETICAL DIRECTORY.
Amos, Chas. Henry, Bagnall
Ardern, Franklyn, Stanley Moor
Bailey, Henry, Houghwood
Ball, James, Bagnall
Ball, Jas., Stone Hole
Ball, Mrs. Ann, Jack Hay Lane
Bayley, Edward Simpson, The Homestead
Bowyer, Arthur, Stockton Brook
Bowyer, Hannah, Houghwood
Brassington, Fred, Bagnall
Brindley, James, Luzlow, Bagnall
Brown, Mrs. Mary, Bagnall
Callear, John, farmer, Greenway Hall Farm
Chadwick, S., Stanley Moor
Challinor, Thos. George, Bagnall
Chaplin, Rev. M., The Parsonage
Chell, Wm. Henry, Clewlows Bank
Cliffe, Samuel, farmer
Collier, Elizabeth, Stanley-road
Corbishley, Jos., Stanley Moss
Corbishley, Joseph, farmer
Cornes, Mrs., Bagnall
Dean, George, Bagnall

Edge, Thomas, Bagnall
Finney, John, farmer
Firkin, Isaac, Stanley Moss
Glover, Jno., Croney Bank, Bagnall
Goodall, Wm., Washer Meadows
Gratton, James, Stanley Pool
Hassall, Joseph, Thorney Edge
Hill, Hannah, Bagnall
Hodgkinson, James, Jack Hay Lane
Holland, Wm., Stanley Moss
Howarth, John, Stanley Mill
Hulme, Fredk., Martin, Stockton Brook
Hulme, Herbert, farmer
Hunt, George, Canal-side, Stockton Brook
Jackson, Enoch, Wm., Salters Well
Jackson, Ernest, Bagnall
Jebb, Wm. T. D., Bagnall
Jodrell, J Holly Bush Inn (F.L.), Stockton Brook
Johnson, George, farmer
Keates, Jno. Alfonso, St. Chad's House
Kilfoil, Frederick Wm., Stanley Moss
Kilfoil, Walter, Bagnall
Killett, Chas., Police Station
Lomas, Ann, farmer
Lomas, William H., farmer
Lomas, Wm. Henry, Grove House
Maddox, Wm., Stanley -lane
Matthews, Albert Edward, Lime Tree Farn
Matthews, George M., Bagnall
Matthews, William, farmer
Mitchell, Thomas, Bagnall
Moore, Arthur, Stafford Arms Inn
Moore, Benj., Stanley Moss
Moore, George, Stanley-road, Bagnall

Mountford, Mrs. Mary, Bagnall
Myatt, James, farmer
Myatt, Jno., Stanley Moor
Myatt, Mrs., Jack Hay-lane
Newton, Robt., Salters Well
Nixon, Vincent Jno., Hospital
Oulsman, Wm. Jno., Bagnall
Parry, Thomas, Mowbray
Parry, Thomas M.
Perkin, Wm. Tomkin, Bagnall
Perkin, William, farmer.
Poulson, Jno., Stanley-road
Preston, Walter Thos. Jack Hay-lane
Price, George, Light Oaks
Prowse, Robt., Greenfields
Reeves, Wm., Jack Hay-lane
Rowley, Arthur, Bagnall
Salt, Wm. J., Clewlows Bank
Scott, Jno., Stanley-road
Sherratt, Jno., Manor Farm
Stanway, Albert, Bagnall
Steventon, Thomas, Bagnall
Stoddard, Fanny, Stanley-road
Sylvester, Chas., Bagnall
Sylvester, Chas., Haythorn, Bagnall
Sylvester, Chas., Bagnall
Sylvester, Walter, Bagnall
Tallon, James, Bagnall
Thomson, Thomas, Sunnyside Farm
Tomkinson, James, Stockton Brook
Turner, Phœbe, Stanley-road
Unwin, Henry, farmer
Wardle, Jno., Greenway Cottage
Wardle, Wm., Greenway Hall
Wilshaw, John, The Bungalow Farm
Woolley, Edwin, Bagnall Grange
Yarwood, Jno., Jack Hay-lane
Yarwood, Jno., T., Lime Tree Farm

tied to a sign post and flayed alive. The Murhall family occupied the hall until 1762. During the 1800s the Myatt family lived there and by 1881 the Keates family were in residence.

There are still many noteworthy buildings in the village to-day. The Stafford Arms is thought to be one of the oldest hostelries in Staffordshire. Some of the stone work in the old stables (now a bar) is believed to date from the 16th century. During the 1940s the old stables were used for storage, and could be entered via the old stone porch. The porch had tiny windows and stone seats. In those days there was no outer door to the porch and the children from the school would shelter from the rain as they waited for the bus to take them home.

Next door to The Stafford Arms is St. Chad's House. It was known as the clergy house and is thought to be three hundred years old. Originally it was the property of the Reverend S.H. Owen. The panelling in the main room is believed to have come from the old pews in St. Chad's Church. Over the fireplace in that room are inscribed the words, 'Fear God. Honour the King'.

Another old property in the village is Bank Farm, dating from the 16th century. William Adams lived at the farm from1794 until 1810. He owned the corn mill near to Stanley Pool. This mill was shown to be in existence on the Yates map of 1775. It was operated by the stream that now runs into Stanley Pool.

Old Mills Lane and Pool Meadows farm derive their names from the old corn mill. The last owner of the corn mill was Mr. George Coxen Jones. He resided at Horton Lodge from 1912 until1916 and he owned a number of properties in the Bagnall area. The corn mill was destroyed when the dam at Old Mills Fields burst and the mill wheel was carried by the force of the water nearly a quarter of a mile down towards Stanley Moss, almost opposite to Stanley Head Farm. After the waters abated, the ditches around the fields were packed with fish. The mill was finally demolished and some of the stones were used at Bank Farm  for out buildings.

Lawn Farm was occupied in 1791 and Greenfield Farm dates back to 1666. Jackhaye Farm goes back to 1652 and Old hall Farm and Manor Farm were occupied in 1851 according to the census.

Greenway Hall is on the outskirts of the village. It was once owned by Judge Bradshaw, who as president of the High Court of Justice, helped to sentence Charles I to the scaffold. Judge Bradshaw was a native of Marple near Stockport. He served his clerkship at Congleton and was High Steward and Recorder for Newcastle. When the old Greenway Hall was demolished in 1880, blood money was supposed to have been concealed in the building, but none was ever found. A farmhouse now occupies the site.

When the census was held in 1851 the enumerator appointed as the superintendent registrar for the area was Thomas Stone of Holly Grove Farm, Bagnall. He was 45 years old and his farm covered an area of 6 acres. He lived at Holly Grove with his wife Ann (aged 42), a servant (aged 15) and an agricultural labourer. The census was held in March and Thomas had to deliver all the census forms himself. Then in April he collected all the forms in again. As a number of the villagers were illiterate he had to fill in the forms for them using a 'graphite' stick, as pencils were not introduced until 1900.

When the statistics were correlated it emerged that the males outnumbered the females by 6.4%, and it was a youngish community. In 1851 there were 70 families living in the village, and there were a few uninhabited houses. Life expectancy was lower than to-day and few villagers lived to the age of 65. The occupations listed in the census included agricultural workers, blacksmiths, crate makers, policemen, tailors, wheelwrights, colliers, stone masons at quarries at Bagnall and Baddeley Edge, boatmen and butchers. The females were servants, dressmakers, washerwomen and dairy maids.

St. Chad's Church was recorded on Saxton's map of 1577 and the Morden map of 1727. It was described then as a small wooden structure with a wooden tower. In his *Topographical History of Staffordshire* Pitt describes the church as *"being in a ruinous state, standing in a pastoral field. It might be mistaken for a small barn but for the wooden belfry, containing a small solitary bell. The east end is propped up by a piece of timber."* It was rebuilt in the 19th century. The tower and nave of the present church were completed in 1834. It is recorded in *White's Directory of Staffordshire* that the cost was £520.

The church was a curacy annexed to Bucknall, and Bagnall was described at that time as being in the Totmonslow Hundred in the Manor of Horton. The chancel was added in 1880. Nothing is known of the wall fixtures in the tower upon which are printed the ten commandments, the Lord's Prayer and the Creed. Originally there was a gallery in the Church - no doubt where small instruments were played during the services.

Some windows were made with glass from Amiens. The window above the Lord's Table shows St. Chad in the middle, with Faith holding a crown of thorns and a cross, and Hope on the other side holding an anchor. The pews are Georgian, but the choir stalls are of a much later date. The two murals on the walls were painted in 1881 by a local artist, John Thorley, and are copies of cartoons by Raphael.

The mural on the South wall depicts the death of Ananias (Acts 4 &5) and on the North wall is the Miraculous Draught of Fishes (Luke 5). The present organ dates from 1824 and it was installed at St. Chad's in 1925. To begin with the organ was powered by a lad squeezing some bellows at the back of the instrument. During the 1920s the church was heated by a coke boiler down in the cellar under the building. The late Vera Sutton sometimes spoke of how she had helped her mother, Mrs Grosvenor, to push wheel barrows filled with coke down the Church path to the cellar to keep the old boiler going.

The stone column in the churchyard close by the porch is all that remains of a sundial. The top stone is dated 1771. During the early 1930s/40s the single church bell was tolled faithfully each Sunday in the morning and before the evening services, by a man known as Rafe, who never appeared to miss a single Sunday.

During the early 19th century no cars would have been seen in the village and the Church had no electricity. The choir and the congregation had to rely on oil lamps. A boy had to stand and blow the bellows at the back of the organ to make it work. At Christmas the choir would be out for four nights visiting the local cottages, farms and pubs. At that time, any money they collected was divided amongst themselves, the men receiving twice as much as the boys. The choir had its own 'six a side' football team. They gave concerts in aid of the organ fund and enjoyed day outings to North Wales, catching the train at Bucknall station.

The ancient cross on the village green is pre-Norman. At one time it was common practice to hold fairs in the churchyards. The cross at Bagnall once stood opposite the Stafford Arms until the Rev. Samuel Herbert Owen had it placed on the stone base in its present position on The Green. The fact that it is a wheel cross - a Celtic cross - proves it was a 'market' or 'barter' cross and obviously markets were held there.

The villagers always liked to celebrate special occasions. In his book *Olde Leeke*, 1891, M.H. Miller wrote that Mr Salt, the oldest inhabitant of Bagnall, recalled that the patriotic parishioners of Bagnall red-lettered the conclusion of the peace following the Battle of Waterloo with a peace celebration bowling match on the village bowling green. Mr Salt was only five at the time, but he remembered it well and there are records of a bowling match being held in 1815 between Leek and Moorlands and a Potteries Team.

May Day Festivals were celebrated in the village in 1861. It is recorded that 150 people sat down to tea at the Stafford Arms Inn. Mr and Mrs Myatt were the host and hostess. The meal was followed by a quadrille band and dances. The *Staffordshire Advertiser* of May 4th 1861 stated that, *"So great was the enjoyment that it is contemplated to make the recurrence of May Day a joyous festival as in the days of yore in this township."* Further May Day festivals were recorded in 1863, 1870 and 1875.

'Harvest Home' celebrations were held in 1863. The *Staffordshire Advertiser* stated, *"A majority of farmers in the township of Bagnall have determined to celebrate the securing of the late harvest by regaling their servants with roast beef, plum pudding and good strong ale. A procession was formed at Greenway Hall. It was led by the Burslem Rifle Corps Band and two labourers carrying a sheaf of corn. Divine service was held in the Church led by Rev T. Biggins. This was followed by dinner, tea and dancing."*

Obviously the villagers worked hard, but knew how to enjoy themselves.

As can be seen Bagnall was a thriving community and it comes as no surprise to learn that in 1873 the local Board of Education expressed their concern about the education of the children in the village. It was decided that a school was needed.

The Stafford Arms at Bagnall. (Present day).

The Stafford Arms in 1910, taken from a postcard reprint, *courtesy of Elton Prints, Packamoor.*

The scene in winter.

*Courtesy of Mr T.W. Mountford.*

The cottages on Springs Bank.

*Courtesy of Mr T.W. Mountford.*

St. Chad's House today.

Springs Bank in the 1930s.

St. Chad's Church, Bagnall. (Present day).

The verse above the doorway at St. Chad's:
'TIS THE HOUSE OF PRAYER - GO IN.
'TIS THE CHRISTIANS HOME BY RIGHT.
FIND SOME NOOK, CONFESS THY SIN
AND GO FORTH IN JESUS' MIGHT.

St. Chad's Church in 1910.

Two murals decorate the walls of St. Chad's Church, *The Miraculous Draught of Fishes*. Luke 5 v 1-11. seen here and *The Death of Ananias*. Acts 4 v 11. They were painted in 1881 by a local artist, John Thorley and are copies of Raphael's work.

The Interior of the Church in 1920.
The mural of *The Last Supper* can be
seen on the wall to the left of the pulpit.
It was painted over during restoration
work in the 1960s.

St. Chad's organ was built in 1924.
It was installed and
dedicated in 1925.
At the dedication a recital was
given by Mr. W. F. Rogers.

The Green, Bagnall, and the Butter Cross.

The Sun Dial in St. Chad's Churchyard.

The Butter Cross.

Bagnall Hall.  The initials J.M. and the date 1603 are inscribed over the doorway
John and Jane Murrall lived there at that time.

The Springs in 1930.

The same scene but with a motor-bike and sidecar.

Bagnall Village in the 1930s.

There were stations at Stockton Brook and Endon on the Stoke to Leek line.

Bagnall Hall from The Green.

The Monks' Way looking towards the road from Bagnall to Werrington.

The Monks' Way also known as The Stumps,
looking towards Jack Haye Lane and Woodhead.

The Monks' Way was known by the locals as The Stumps, and was the old road
from Hulton Abbey to Bagnall and beyond.

An old postcard of the Cross.

Bagnall Grange was originally an outlying grange to Hulton Abbey with a corn mill. The Grange was home to the Hulme family in the 1700s who also owned the mill.

Moor Hall was once a moated farmhouse.

**KEATS BROTHERS,**

Houghwood Quarries, nr. Bagnall, Stoke-on-Trent, *20 april* 18 *83*

*To Messrs Challinor & Co Leek*

Bagnall and Stanley have had busy stone quarries.
The area has also gained a reputation for its nurseries

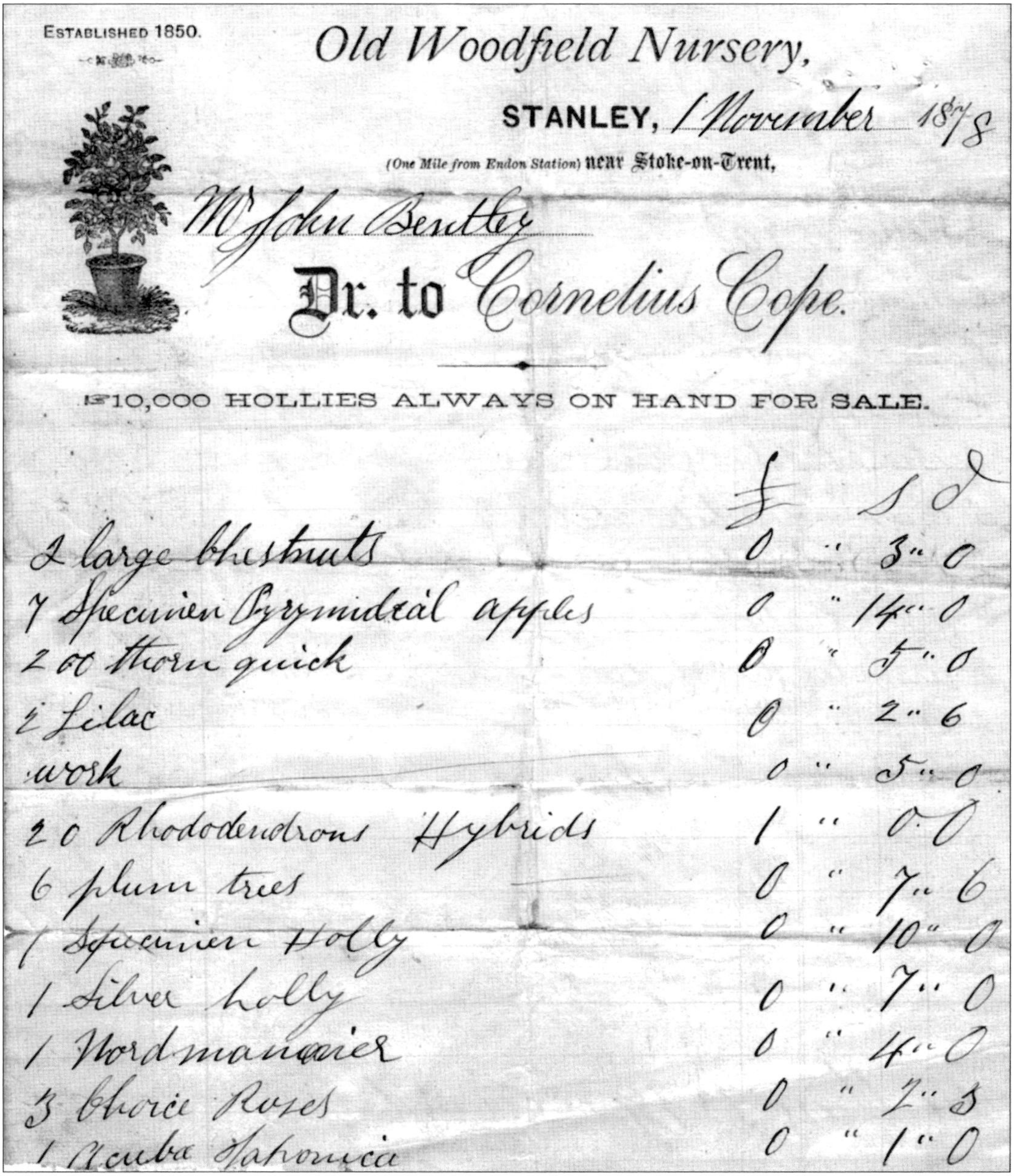

ESTABLISHED 1850.

*Old Woodfield Nursery,*

**STANLEY,** *1 November* 18*78*

(One Mile from Endon Station) **near Stoke-on-Trent,**

*Mr John Bentley*

**Dr. to** *Cornelius Cope.*

10,000 HOLLIES ALWAYS ON HAND FOR SALE.

| | £ | s | d |
|---|---|---|---|
| 2 large chestnuts | 0 | 3 | 0 |
| 7 Specimen Pyramidal apples | 0 | 14 | 0 |
| 200 thorn quick | 0 | 5 | 0 |
| 1 Lilac | 0 | 2 | 6 |
| work | 0 | 5 | 0 |
| 20 Rhododendrons Hybrids | 1 | 0 | 0 |
| 6 plum trees | 0 | 7 | 6 |
| 1 Specimen Holly | 0 | 10 | 0 |
| 1 Silver holly | 0 | 7 | 0 |
| 1 Nordmaniaier | 0 | 4 | 0 |
| 3 choice Roses | 0 | 7 | 3 |
| 1 Aucuba Japonica | 0 | 1 | 0 |

Jack Haye Farm. The window on the gable end of the building was probably blocked up because of the window tax.

Although the deeds go back to 1652 the date over the doorway (below) is 1675

Luzlow Farm, below, was listed in 1871 as the Dog and Partridge.

# LUZLOW, NEAR BAGNALL,
## STAFFORDSHIRE.

---

## MR. J. OAKES ASH

Will offer for Sale by Auction,

AT THE WIND-MILL INN, WERRINGTON.

# ON THURSDAY, AUG. 11th, 1898,

*AT 5 FOR 6 O'CLOCK P.M. SUBJECT TO CONDITIONS.*

---

### LOT 1.

# ALL THAT COMPACT FARM

Situate at Luzlow, consisting of a substantial Farmhouse, with suitable and convenient Outbuildings, and the following Closes of Meadow and Pasture Land, all lying together, and within a ring fence.

| No. on Plan. | Cultivation. | | | | A. | R. | P. |
|---|---|---|---|---|---|---|---|
| 718 | Pasture | ... | ... | ... | 1 | 3 | 36 |
| 719 | Pasture | ... | ... | ... | 1 | 3 | 7 |
| 720 | Meadow | ... | ... | ... | 2 | 3 | 18 |
| 721 | Meadow | ... | ... | ... | 2 | 1 | 29 |
| 722 | Meadow | ... | ... | ... | 1 | 1 | 19 |
| 723 | Pasture | ... | ... | ... | 1 | 3 | 16 |
| 729 | Potatoes and Oats | ... | ... | ... | 1 | 1 | 23 |
| | | | | | 13 | 2 | 28 |

This Farm is freehold with the exception of one Field (No. 720) which is copyhold of the Manor of Horton. It is about 3 miles distant from Milton and Bucknall Railway Stations, and adjoins the highways leading respectively from Cellarhead to Leek, and from Cellarhead to Bucknall.

A sale poster and sketch map for Luzlow Farm in 1898.

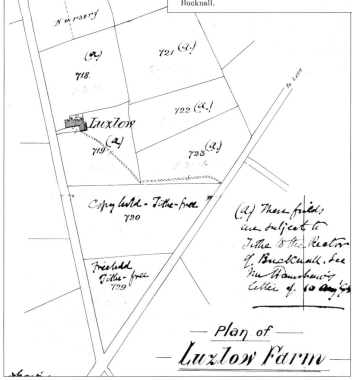

— Plan of —
— Luzlow Farm —

A group outside the school in 1909. Valerie Whittaker's father is 6th from the left on the front row. It is believed that Mr. Parry, (the headmaster) is on the right.

# Chapter 2
# Bagnall School

As the flames leaped into the black night sky, on that fateful night in March 1969, the villagers watched in disbelief as the scorched timbers of Bagnall School fell to the ground. As they watched so many memories came racing back. They couldn't believe that the place where they had spent so much of their childhood days and their leisure hours was now engulfed by this ruthless fire. By the time the local fire brigades had succeeded in quenching the flames, the parts of the building still standing were unsafe and the decision was made to demolish the structure completely.

The building of the school began in 1873 and two classrooms were added later. At first the classrooms were lit by oil lamps and later by electricity. The coke boiler situated under rooms 2 and 3 kept the children warm in Winter.

The school, set up under the authority of the Stoke-upon-Trent School Board, was opened in April 1874. The chair of the School Board was the Reverend Sir Lovelace Stamer, the Rector of the Stoke Parish & later Bishop of Shrewsbury. The event was recorded in the *Staffordshire Advertiser* 2nd May 1874:

*'STOKE SCHOOL BOARD. OPENING OF BAGNALL SCHOOL.*
*On Monday this school was formally opened in the presence of a considerable number of residents in Bagnall. The Rev. Sir L.T. Stamer, Bart. was accompanied by Messrs Gimson, Stoker, Rhead and Stubbs, members, and Mr Thomas, clerk. After congratulating the ratepayers of Bagnall on the completion of their school, the Chairman remarked that the proceedings of the School board during the first three years of its existence had been marked by the evident desire to do justice to every portion of the large district they had to provide for. In the centres of the population the Board had abstained from building, they had hired rooms, which though not entirely suitable had proved very useful as temporary schools.'*

Before the school and the hiring of rooms, some children were educated at a number of dame schools - the dame school house at Werrington can still be seen.

In keeping with many of the buildings in the village such as the church, the Stafford Arms and St Chad's House, the school was built with millstone grit blocks, which were quarried locally. This stonework gave it a rather rugged characteristic. Like most schools in that era the windows were high, so that the children would not be tempted to look out and be distracted from their lessons. Over the main doorway, chiselled into the stonework, was the inscription, 'Stoke upon Trent School Board'.

The schoolyard at the front of the building was cobbled making it difficult to walk on and slippery in winter. The school was linked to the headteacher's house by a long shed-like porch. Along the side of the road the school wall was capped with iron railings for safety. These remained during the war years, when a lot of railings were removed from some areas and melted down for armament manufacture. The remains of the railings can still be seen in the wall of the present village hall car park.

On the other side of the porch was an asphalt playground dominated by the building housing the old Victorian toilets. The boys' were on one side, the girls' on the other, and each little cubicle had a wooden seat with a hole in the centre. The effluent simply dropped into a long wooden trench where it accumulated over the weeks. There were no flushing toilets and the stench was unpleasant. In the 1940s they were still as they must have been constructed in 1874. Occasionally the 'Brandy barrel' would arrive and the waste was sucked into the barrel of the vehicle, to be disposed of elsewhere. Most of the children attending the school in the 1930s and 40s were surprised at these lavatories as most by then had flushing ones at home.

To the rear of the main classrooms was the boys' playground, and at the bottom of the girls' playground was a hawthorn bush, where the children would often eat the berries from the tree - 'bread and cheese'. There were many playground games in which to take part: 'The big ship sails on the Alley Alley Oh', 'In and out the Bluebell Windows', 'The Farmer's in his Den', 'Here we go round the Mulberry Bush', 'On the mountain stands a lady', and 'I wrote a letter to my love'. Ball games and skipping games were popular. The children would use their Mums' old clothes lines for ropes and chant rhymes as they skipped. 'Salt, vinegar, mustard, pepper' and 'North Staffs Railway loopline' could be heard echoing around the playground. And there was a season for whips and tops and conkers during the Autumn.

During the 1940s the air raid shelter stood in the caretaker's garden. The concrete roof could be seen standing just above the level of the garden. Today it must be buried somewhere beneath the Village Hall.

The headteachers appointed to the school did not stay long, possibly due to poor pay or the isolated nature of the community.

James Bander, the first headmaster, was appointed in 1874, and stayed at the school for just two years. He had completed his teacher training at Edinburgh Church of Scotland Training College. The school was at that time an all age school taking the little ones in at 4 or 5 years, and they remained at the school until they sought employment. By June 1874 there were 101 children on the roll.

Attendance at the school appears to have been very spasmodic due to illness and poor weather in the winter, and potato and blackberry picking in the Summer months. In June 1875 a number of children were absent as they had attended Baddeley Edge Well Dressing celebrations in Spout Lane.

In February 1875 the *Staffordshire Advertiser* described a concert at the school:

*'On Tuesday an evening concert was given at the new Board School, Bagnall, in aid of the Sunday School in connection with Bagnall Church. There was a large attendance. The programme was sustained by Miss Brown of Hanley whose singing was encored in*

*several instances ...Miss Pointon sang with good effect 'Tis but a little faded flower', and a duet by Messrs Drury and Wright justly merited the encore it received.... The singing of the National Anthem closed a very pleasant entertainment. The proceeds amounted to about £5.'*

In 1876 John William Nicholls was appointed headteacher. He had trained at Chester Training College and he remained at the school for three years, when Samuel and Kate Stevens were appointed. In the 1881 census the people in the school house were listed as:

| Samuel Stevens | Head | Marr. | 40 | Schoolmaster | Born Wilts |
| Kate Stevens | Wife | Marr. | 40 | Schoolmistress | Wilts, Imber |
| Kate E. Stevens | Dau | Single | 19 | Schoolmistress | Northants, Litchborough |
| Harry G Stevens | Son | Single | 16 | Pupil Teacher | Northants, Litchborough |
| Mabel Stevens | Dau | Single | 14 | Scholar | Northants, Litchborough |
| William H Stevens | Son | Single | 11 | Scholar | Nottingham. Upton |
| Edgar A Stevens | Son | Single | 10 | Scholar | Nottingham. Upton |
| Ethel L Stevens | Dau | Single | 6 | Scholar | Oxford. Aston Bampton |
| Agnes O Stevens | Dau | Single | 5 | Scholar | Oxford. Aston Bampton |
| Cecil Stevens | Son | Single | 3 | | Oxford Aston Bampton |
| Frederick Stevens | Son | Single | 1 | | Staffs. Bagnall |
| Sarah Shenton | St. | | 17 | General Servant | Staffs. Wetley Rocks |

When Mr and Mrs Stevens and their family left, there were 134 pupils on the roll at the school. Later in that year, 1881, Mr and Mrs Heal were in charge, and they remained at the school for sixteen years.

There was quite a lot of hardship and poverty in the village at this time. The 1881 census listed the villagers' occupations as, labourers, farm workers, miners etc. Mrs Elizabeth Bass, whilst researching her books about Bucknall and Werrington met Mrs Lily Wheat. She was born in about 1889 and attended Bagnall School when Mr Heal was the headmaster. She was one of twelve children and when the youngest was born her mother died. When she was asked to write down some of her recollections of Bagnall she confessed that she wasn't very good at reading and writing, because instead of attending school she had had to remain at home most of the time to look after all the family. When she married her husband he taught her to read and write a little. She met her husband at a fair and they were married at Wetley Rocks.

In 1897, the year of Queen Victoria's Diamond Jubilee, the children walked in procession to the village cross where five chestnut trees had been planted to mark the occasion. The trees were named Victoria, Helena, Beatrice, Louise and Alice, after five of Victoria's daughters. The children were presented with jubilee mugs and the day ended with a bonfire and fireworks

Mr and Mrs Parry were appointed in 1897 and they remained at the school until 1920. Sadly Mr Parry died whilst still headmaster.

Elizabeth Bass, in *Werrington, Yesterday's Voices*, records some memories of life at the school in Mr Parry's time.  Life wasn't easy for the children!

Mary Jane Harvey (later Mary Jane Dale and buried in St. Chad's churchyard with her husband Nathan) recorded:

"My father was Samuel Harvey.  He was a pitman from Stanley.  My mother was Joyce Brown of Bagnall Grange Farm.

I was born at Eaves Lane but we flitted to Kerry Hill before I got very old.  Mother's uncle Joe farmed Moorside and Kerry Hill together.  We lived downstairs in great big rooms and the house was in such a bad way, the snow came through the roof in winter.  We had two beds in one room.  We slept top to bottom.  It isn't very nice having someone's toe next to your nose.

The roads were bad.  We used to go down the Stumpy Lane to Bagnall.

I went to Bagnall School.  It was a very good school.  You know, there was Big Huntbaches and Little Huntbaches in Hanley.  Big Huntbaches sent Lizzie, their girl, to our school.  She lodged at the school house all week and they fetched her home at  weekends.  She mixed with us, no difference, played hopscotch with us in the yard.  They must have been well off.  She never wore a pinner - she wore a blue dress of good stuff and low shoes.  We'd all got strong boots and clogs.  I wore strong boots, they used to last me twelve months without mending.  I was light on my feet.

We were never late even though we walked from the other side of the common.  The children in the village got the stick for being late.  Teacher Harding was very strict.  We daren't laugh in school.  I never went to a school party.   For one thing I got no clothes,  I only had the frock I went to school in and one pinner.

We used to eat our dinner at school.  Me brother said one day, *"What an we got for dinner?"*  Mother said, *"Jam"*.  We always had jam.  She would get blackberries and make jam to last the whole year.  She would make thirty of forty jars.  She never had to buy jam.

In Summer we all sat outside at the stone cross to eat our dinner.  Someone was monitor and fetched the drinking water in a tin jug from the Springs.  In Winter you had to break the ice before you could get at it for a drink.

One day we thought we'd got a half-holiday so we didn't take any dinner.  We said we hadn't brought our dinner.  It wasn't a half holiday.  They told the teachers, *"Harveys haven't brought their dinner"*. The teachers told us to beg a bit from the other children to pull us through the day.  One child did offer me a bite of cake, but not my brother.  So we went home.

We went back the next morning.  Mrs Parry lived in the school house. She didn't care to give us nothing.  She put us down a standard below for a full week. We had our punishment, then she put us back into our own class.

We played a game of Fox and Hounds one dinner time when it was nice weather.  Once we went too far over the fields, and all the girls were late.  We got the cane.

There was a big pool in front of the Public House at Bagnall.  When it was froz we used to go sliding on it in Winter.

We had no pleasures, we were too poor. We were too poor to have anything. We wanna pampered. We had an orange and apple every Christmas. We always had a plum pudding Mother made.

Margaret Heath (Corbishley):

"I remember my mother telling me about the school when she was there. She lived at Bank Farm at the top of the Springs Bank when she was a girl. The winters were really bad then. Mr Parry was the headmaster at the school, and he was very strict, but kind.

In those days some of the boys wore short trousers and in the Winter he would be so concerned about the cold weather he would wrap brown paper around their legs to keep them warm on the way home.

The children in the top class used real ink to write with and my mother had an accident and spilled quite a lot. She was made to scrub for ages until the stain had been removed. She would take bacon and eggs to school sometimes and the teacher would cook them for her dinner on the stove in Class 1

Mrs Bass also interviewed Mrs Johnson who attended the school in Mr Parry's time:

She had lived in the Light Oaks/Kerry Hill area, and had to walk through the Barn Fields each day to get to school. There were no school dinners in those days, but some days her mother would meet her in the Barn Fields at dinner time and she would give her some bread and butter sandwiches. Sometimes however, her mother didn't have anything to give her and she returned to school feeling hungry and dejected. She would walk home at teatime hoping there would be something to eat when she arrived.

She remembered the big Christmas tree in the school at Christmas time, when loaves of bread were distributed to the poorest children. A plaque in the Church testifies to the distribution of bread to the poor.

Mr Parry taught Geography whilst Mrs Parry took the girls for needlework and taught them how to make patches from two pieces of flannel. One day Mrs Johnson and her sister Nancy were doing their patches and Nancy's work wasn't up to standard. Mrs Parry was not pleased and made Nancy stand at the front of the class. She held the patch up on her back for everyone to see. Nancy's sister (Mrs Johnson) ran up and snatched the patch off Nancy's back. Mrs Parry was extremely angry and marched her to Mr Parry's room where she was promptly given the cane.

A number of reports from His Majesty's Inspectors have survived from Mr Parry's time as head:

W.B. Yarde, HMI 1905:

'_This is a good school. The regulations are carried out in an earnest and intelligent manner and without undue strain. An excellent tone prevails._'

However he continued:

'_The playground which is very small is in a very bad condition. The ventilation_ *should be improved, especially in the classroom where I found the atmosphere very oppressive. The cloakroom and lavatory accommodation are insufficient.  The office accommodation (toilet provision) is quite inadequate for the number of children and there is no provision for infants, nor for the teachers.  The boys offices (toilets) are so near to the schoolroom as to be a source of danger and at times offensive smells are noticed in school.'*

Four years later his report of 1909 stated:

*"It is hoped the girls may take some share in the drawing lessons.  The needlework is well taught, and the mending of garments has not been neglected....... '*

*'The children read with accuracy and good expression and follow the subject well. Seeing that the upper class children have more than average intelligence and ability it would be wise to give more time to silent reading, and the training of the children in habits of private study.'*

Mr Parry died whilst holding the post of headmaster and a brass plaque was placed in Class 2 to his memory.

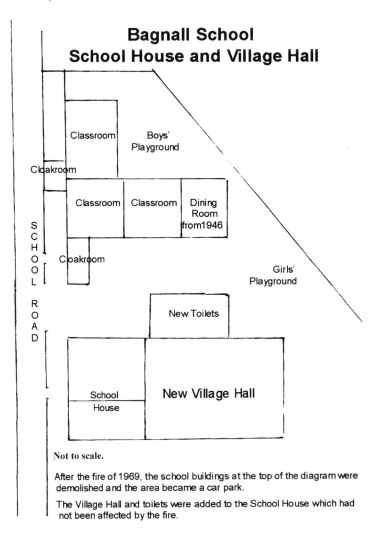

**Bagnall School
School House and Village Hall**

Classroom

Boys' Playground

Cloakroom

Classroom | Classroom | Dining Room from1946

Cloakroom

Girls' Playground

New Toilets

School House | New Village Hall

SCHOOL ROAD

**Not to scale.**

After the fire of 1969, the school buildings at the top of the diagram were demolished and the area became a car park.

The Village Hall and toilets were added to the School House which had not been affected by the fire.

A school photograph taken in 1909.

Some more early photos of Bagnall School.

Christmas at Bagnall School in 1910.

An Early photograph of
Bagnall School.

A painting of Bagnall School and the School House by Michael Bond.

The same site today.

The Village Hall was built on to the School House in the early 1970s.

The School House today.

A group outside the bike shed at Bagnall School in 1915.
Betty Sylvester is at the end of the middle row on the right hand side.
Cissie Brassington is wearing a hat on the back row.

A school photograph taken in 1900. Vernon Steele, the late Mary Wain's and Margaret Davis's
father, is 4th from the left on the second row from the front.

# Chapter 3
# Other Schools in the Area

Bagnall Hospital opened in 1890 and consisted of a number of wooden buildings. It was built and used as an isolation hospital - it was used to house smallpox patients. In 1903 severe gales caused damage to the roof and to chimney stacks and the decision was made to replace the wooden structures with a more permanent building. There were a number of objections, particularly as there had been outbreaks of smallpox in the village in the past. However a new building was built and opened in 1906. In 1919 it was proposed that instead of smallpox patients the hospital should now cater for children suffering from tuberculosis. These children had been treated at Bucknall hospital prior to the new arrangement.

Bagnall Hospital.

By 1920 a school had opened in the hospital grounds to educate these children. The school was held in a wooden hut and one of the first teachers was Miss Lucy Jones. In 1948 Miss Kath Jury was appointed as the headmistress.

The Hospital School. Kath Jury:

"In 1948 I had seen the advertisement for qualified teachers for the Bagnall Hospital School, and I decided to apply. I was invited for an interview and on the appointed day I caught the Milton Service bus at Yew Tree for the short journey to the hospital. On the bus I met a friend of mine, Kath Stokes, from Trent Vale. We started talking and to our astonishment we discovered we were both going to the hospital to be interviewed for the same job. The interviews took place and finally I was chosen to be the headteacher with Kath Stokes as the other teacher.

I had been trained to teach infants and when I started teaching I had done supply work at various schools in the locality. At one stage I taught the older children at Moorland Road Boys' School in Burslem. When I was appointed to the hospital school I was teaching at Carmountside Primary School. My time at the Bagnall Hospital School was some of the happiest days of my life.

The children we taught hadn't actually got tuberculosis but they had been in close contact with people who were suffering from the disease, and their time with us varied considerably. We taught them whilst they were in their beds. Miss Burke was the matron at that time and she was very strict. We seemed to have rice pudding for lunch 365 days in the year. It would arrive in a large bucket, and we had to serve it out to the children. The food was generally poor and there never seemed to be enough to go round. We often had to take food from one child's plate to give to someone else.

One year there was great excitement when Councillor Eardley presented the children with a real donkey from the Smallthorne and Bradeley Community Association. We kept it in the hospital grounds, but one day it simply disappeared. We never managed to discover what had happened to it.

At Christmas we always had a Christmas concert. We trained the children for the concert and at dinner times Kath Stokes would sit by the pot stove in the school hut to make all the costumes. We obtained the material as remnants from the market stalls in Hanley. The children's parents were invited on the day of the concert, but they were kept waiting outside by matron whilst her special visitors had been seated at the front It wasn't always pleasant to have to queue up, especially if it was raining or snowing.

On Sundays the curate from St. Chad's would come in to take the Sunday School, but if he wasn't able to get along I did it, or sometimes the matron would take the service.

A number of doctors came to visit the children each week. One of the nicest was a lady doctor called Dr John. She always took such an interest in their welfare and their progress. As I said they were happy days for us and we remained at the school until 1958 when the children were transferred to Bucknall Hospital.

The Sunday School at Bagnall

The foundation stone for St. Chad's Sunday School was laid in 1909 by H. Heath. Many children from the local area attended. During the late 1930s when Joyce Rowley first went to Sunday School, she walked along Baddeley Edge to the Methodist Chapel there, but Mrs Brown who ran the Hollies Private School suggested that she might like to change to the Bagnall Sunday School. She did and thus started a long association with St. Chad's Sunday School.

Miss Stanway was leading the Sunday School at that time assisted by Alice Wain and Bertha Tatton. At the age of 14 Joyce was invited to teach at the Sunday School. When the children met there would be an introductory session with hymn singing etc. and then the children would divide into groups according to age and listen to bible stories, study the bible and partake in various activities. Often they were given small text cards with appropriate verses from the Bible. These were always attractively illustrated, and the children were always keen to collect them.

There were outings to Congleton Park, Dudley Zoo and to the beautiful gardens at

Trentham, where the children could ride on the miniature railway that ran along the side of the lake and play on the swings.  There were parties and the annual prize giving.  The children won prizes for good attendance and the little ones would receive consolation prizes.  These would be books or certificates.

The children looked forward to the Sunday School Anniversary when they would dress in their finery and sing and give readings.  A number of people helped at the Sunday School over the years: Joyce Rowley, Marion Ford, Margaret Corbishley, Doris Hemming, Kath Stokes, Mr Allan, Sandra Glover, Joan Greasley, Joan Thorley, Alison Morrall and her twin sister, Christine Baigent, Margaret Adams, Sheila Glover, Brian Sweatmore and Bob Shufflebottom were a few.

During the 1930s a Bible class for adults met in Mrs Brown's House in Jack Haye Lane.  Later Bible classes for older children were held in St. Chad's Church and in Bagnall School. Alan Myatt, Anne Lewis and Roger Hampson worked with the Pathfinder group

The Hollies at Light Oaks

When the Hollies School was first established in the early 1900s it occupied premises in Prince's Road at Newcastle.  Then the Bird family, who ran the school, moved to Baddeley Edge and the school was housed in the Baptist Chapel in Fowler's Lane.  By the late 1930s the school had moved to Jack Haye Lane, Light Oaks.  Children attended the school from Light Oaks, Yew Tree, Milton, Bucknall and Abbey Hulton.  There were also a few boarders from time to time. Locally it was always known as Miss Bird's, but it was run jointly for a majority of the time by Miss Bird and her sister Mrs Brown. Other teachers helped from time to time.  The school eventually closed in the late 1960s.

The Hollies School was a small private school at Light Oakes from about 1930 to the late 1960s this picture of the school and pupils was taken in the 1930s and is from Mrs Dorothy M. Norris's book *The Hollies School* published in 2004 and still available from local bookshops or direct from the author on 01484 851976.

The children gathered to celebrate the coronation of King George VI and Queen Elizabeth.

Another view of the coronation service held on The Green in 1937.

# Chapter 4
# Mr Charles Hargreaves, Headteacher 1920-44

Mr Charles Hargreaves was appointed to Bagnall School in 1920 and had the distinction of being the longest serving headteacher when he retired in 1944. To begin with he lived in the school house, but later he moved with his wife and daughter to a bungalow off Fowler's Lane at Light Oaks.

Former pupils recall that he was a short, stocky man with spectacles. He had a reputation for being very strict. To begin with he taught the senior pupils in the large Classroom 1, but later he had to share this room with another teacher. This room also boasted a gallery at one end, so groups of children could be taken up there for some of the time, giving them a little more space and privacy.

Dorothy Welch (Shenton):

"I remember going to register at Bagnall School. It was a beautiful day. Mr Hargreaves had a short fuse and often caned the pupils. His cane was one that made a noise before it struck. In fact he gave Margaret Clowes the cane because her handwriting was so bad. I never had the cane.

I also remember Arthur Mould carrying his little sister Jean on his back up Clewlows Bank. He was always getting the cane for some misdemeanour or other. I remember Miss Brassington shouting at me when I went to gather the register.

The gallery was in the top room and we had to climb the steps to it."

V.F. Podmore:

"I would be five when I started to school, which would be in January 1920. I can remember holding my sister's hand as we walked down Lawn Lane (Thorney Edge Road) on my way to my first day at school. Walking in those days was a way of life.

We entered the school playground through gates leading from the roadside, with the headmaster's house on our right, turned left up a few stone steps and entered the school through doors which lead into the cloakrooms. There were three classrooms. The first one had a long rope hanging from high up on the wall. This was attached to the school bell on the roof. A pupil was selected to be responsible for pulling on the rope to ring the bell a short time before classes started in the morning and again in the afternoon.

School would start at 9am and finish at 3.30pm. I think holidays were five weeks in the Summer and a week at both Easter and Christmas. No half term breaks then. We did attend a short service at St. Chad's Church during Lent.

All the classrooms were furnished with wooden desks and forms. At the back of the top room was a large stove which was totally inefficient and inadequate especially during severe winter weather.

The toilets were in a corner of the back playground and they weren't water closets.

The teachers, apart from the headmaster, Mr Hargreaves, were all females: Misses Stanistreet, Marshall and Brassington.

When I was six we moved to live at Basnett's Wood at Endon. I still went to the school at Bagnall. I had to walk across the fields to the mill at Stanley Moss, then up Clewlow's Bank to Bagnall. It was quite a journey for a six year old, and the weather wasn't very good at times."

In fact during the Summer of 1927 the weather conditions in North Staffordshire were particularly bad. During the last week in June and the first week in July there were terrible thunder storms following a heat wave and Stanley Pool overflowed flooding Stanley Moss, Endon and Stockton Brook. The children returning from Bagnall School in the early afternoon had to be carried through the floods. Many people, in the area, had to leave their homes until the water had subsided. At the other side of the hill, the stream that ran through the fields and woods at the side of the Yew Tree, on its journey to Milton, became badly flooded and cascaded down Bagnall Bank. Rocks and debris were carried along in the flood and culverts burst. Florence Chetwin in her book *Milton Memories* recalled how the children there remembered seeing rhubarb, cabbages, dead hens and even hen cotes being carried along by the surging waters. Miss Stanistreet lived in Milton and she would have experienced great difficulty in getting to the school at Bagnall to teach her class.

Millie Hilditch (Fowler):

"Mr Hargreaves was my headmaster and he lived in the schoolhouse in those days. His wife would come across to school to take the girls for needlework. I was 10 when she taught me and at the end of the lesson she would always say, *"Fold your garments up girls."* It's just one of those things that you remember!

I will always remember the tea party we had to celebrate the coronation of King George VI and Queen Elizabeth, because afterwards we were allowed to keep the coronation mugs we drank our tea from.

We held our sports days in the field by the side of Old Hall Farm and I was so proud when I was presented with a green leather purse for winning one of the races. We played rounders on the small green in School Road.

At that time Rose Cottage in School Road served as a post office and sweet shop. Mrs Hill ran the shop and she always looked very impressive in her long black dress. I little thought when I was a child that many years later I would return to the school as the school secretary."

The HMI report of June 28th 1933 stated that:

*'The removal of the gallery from the largest classroom has allowed the headteacher to re-arrange his school, and the senior division, comprising 60 pupils at present, is taught by 2*

The drive to Addlestone Villa, Stanley, after the flood.

Eddie Kilfoil and Mr Vickers are in the group inspecting the flood damage at Hercules Mill, Stanley, 1927.

Stanley Pool overflowed on 12th July 1927.  This shows the flood damage at the bottom of Stanley Bank.

Flood damage at the bottom of Bagnall Bank in 1927.  The stream that runs past Yew Tree house flooded.

*teachers in this room. 31 children are in the small room.'*

The HMI report 7 May 1936 said that space was at a premium and numbers were increasing:

*'It would be helpful if more attention was given to some speech training activities of a stimulating character.*

*The Infants work under congested conditions. 36 on roll and they are taught in a small room with a floor space of less than 300 sq. feet.*

*The headmaster should now make more generous arrangements for instruction in Physical Training, craft occupations for the boys and drawing for the girls.'*

In 1939 the new secondary school opened at Endon and the senior children were transferred there. The children now had more space and the Infants were moved to the much larger classroom at the far end of the school, which became Miss Stanistreet's domain for many years.

George Bowler born 1917:

"I played in the football team when Mr Hargreaves was the headmaster at Bagnall. It was called the 'Amber and Blacks' and we did really well.

One memory that stands out is when Mr Hargreaves gave a number of boys a plot of land in the caretaker's garden and encouraged them to grow vegetables in it."

Rachel Cartwright (Unwin):

"We lived at Greenfield and walked to school down the Stumps. It was quite a journey for a five year old and we walked in all types of weather. The school bell started to ring at about 8.45, and when we arrived at school we had to line up in the yard for our shoes to be inspected to make sure they were clean (after our three mile walk to school!) In 1935 we celebrated the Jubilee of King George V and Queen Mary by parading up to the village and standing round the cross to sing hymns. In 1937 we celebrated the coronation of George VI and Queen Elizabeth. Each child had a mug with the Bagnall Cross stamped on the bottom. One of the hymns we sang was 'I vow to thee my country'.

On nice Spring days we were taken down to the Houghwood or to Bagnall Springs.

At break times we had little bottles of milk, and we paid $2^{1}/_{2}$ d per week for them.

In Miss Stanistreet's room at the lower end of the school there was an open fire and she loved to strand with her back to the fire and warm her bottom. She was also particularly fond of chewing those little black liquorice pieces we used to buy in those days.

At Rose Cottage in School Road, Granny Hill kept the village post office. She also sold sweets and chocolates and as we opened the creaky door of the shop we would notice all the sweets and chocolates stacked up her stairs. We were never quite sure how she managed to get up to bed.

One day Miss Brassington came to school in a beautifully knitted cornflower blue suit. Obviously she was dressed in readiness for a special occasion after school. Some of the girls must have annoyed her and Miss Brassington rushed up the aisle between the desks to deal with the offenders.  Sadly she caught her stockings on one of the desks, and when she inspected the ladders she wasn't too pleased.

Mr Hargreaves, the headmaster, had a moustache and he often twisted the ends of it. He always wore a fob watch and chain, and when he talked to you he always put his hands in his pockets and jangled his keys and loose change.  My mother had always stressed that I must never accept lifts from strangers.  One day I was in Milton and a car drew up at the side of me.  Mr Hargreaves was driving and he offered me a lift to Light Oaks, but I refused to get into his car because mother's words rang out in my ears.

I left Bagnall School in 1939 to attend the new school at Endon."

In 1935 George V and Queen Mary celebrated the Silver Jubilee of their coronation. The event was marked by the children parading from the school, with flags flying, to the Cross on the Green, where a special service was conducted by the Rev. Leslie Shone.  The King died the following year.  Following the abdication of Edward VIII, his brother, Albert succeeded to the throne and was crowned  George VI at Westminster Abbey in May 1937. Again a royal occasion was celebrated by the school with a procession to the Green and a special service.

Lessons in the school yard 1934. Rachel Unwin is the young pupil holding the stick.

Freda Stubbs:

"I have vivid memories of my sister running out of school into the road one day and being knocked down by a passing vehicle.  She was taken to hospital and anxious days followed, until she was well enough to return home.

I also remember how we children wore oak leaves on our lapels on 'Oak Apple Day'."
Valerie Whittaker (Sylvester):

"I started at the school at the beginning of Coronation year, 1937, when I was just five years old. Miss Stanistreet was my first teacher. Our class shared a cloakroom with the second class. We had our own peg for our coat but I don't think we had our name on it.

The classroom was the smallest in the school. I suppose there were about 24 pupils in it. We sat in desks and two desks were joined together. I sat by my best friend Audrey. We have been friends since we were two and we are still friends!

I remember a coloured picture that was near to the door. It was of two children near a gate where foxgloves were in flower. There was a poem written on it. There were pots of red and pink geraniums on the window sills. Miss Stanistreet asked my father if he could look after the plants during the long Summer holiday, which he did because he was a keen gardener.

I can't remember her lessons, except playing with plasticine in the afternoon. Miss Stanistreet suggested that the plasticine would keep soft if we put it in a tin and my Grandfather used to save his cigarettes tins to send to school, as they were just the right size. I remember learning to knit in the second class. I knitted a bonnet for my doll with a scarf to match in bright red wool. I enjoyed learning to read and write and do arithmetic.

The highlight of the year was the Coronation celebration. It was in May and we walked into the village and lined up by the cross on the village green. Since we were the smallest children we stood in the front row. We each carried a small union jack, which we waved as we walked along. It must have been quite a cool day as we wore coats and hats.

The Rev'd Shone conducted a service at the cross. Other villagers came to it too. The Rev'd Shone was the curate at St. Chad's Church. Later he was to marry the teacher who took the second class. Miss Leese. After the service we went back to the school, where we had a party. There was no T.V. then but we saw the black and white photographs in the newspaper. I was particularly interested in his two daughters, our present Queen and her sister, then known as Princess Margaret Rose. She was just a little bit older than myself and Princess Elizabeth was a little older than my sister Kathleen.

One memory I have was when I was six, and we had just returned to school after the Christmas holiday, and I slipped on the recently oiled floor and chipped one of my teeth. I must have been upset, so I was taken to the headmaster. He took me on his knee and I stayed there for a while - I doubt whether that would happen these day!

My Grandfather was a school manager, so I was very proud when he came to see round the school from time to time.

I lived three quarters of a mile from the school and I usually walked through the fields with other children in the morning, but caught the bus at dinner time, home and back again - the time was so short. I would buy weekly tickets on a Monday. Our mothers didn't come to meet us from school. We made our own way, either through the barn fields or over the golf links. I stayed at the school for three years, and then I left to go to another school."

Audrey Rennie (Shenton):

"Before the Secondary School was built at Endon, just prior to the second world war (1939-1945), pupils normally went to Bagnall School from the age of five until they left to start work at age fourteen. The odd one went to Grammar School at age eleven. The teachers at that time were, starting from the Infants upwards were: Effie Stanistreet, Nancy Leese (who married the local curate Leslie Shone), Cis Brassington, Peggy Mathers, Charlie Hargreaves.

The pupils were located as follows: Infants in the small bottom room with Juniors in the large middle room with a dividing partition (2 classes) and the Seniors in 2 classes at each end of the large top room.

We normally walked to school from Light Oaks, where I lived. When it was too wet we went by bus. We used to get a small pad of tickets known as 'Weeklies', very pale green tickets with a red $^1/2$d printed on the front.

The boys and girls had separate playgrounds with the boys at the back by the fields and the girls at the side of the schoolhouse garden. The toilets in those days used to be at the bottom of the playgrounds, and were emptied by a wagon, which came round once a week.

In the playground we played games like 'Stag', 'Hot Rice', 'Releavo' and musical circle party games where we sang 'Nuts in May'. There were the seasons for top and whip, marbles, hopscotch, ball games, skipping -we never got bored.

We used to get regular visits from the district nurse to inspect our hair for nits and periodic visits from a doctor and a dentist. Whenever the dentist came I remember the singing lessons to cover up the screams, as no pain killers were used then. I remember one year when I had badly neglected my teeth. The result was 1 filling and 4 extractions. It taught me a lesson. Since then I never eat with out cleaning my teeth. It is a standing joke in my family. If I was asked about a last request before a firing squad, my answer would be *"can I clean my teeth?"*

The second world war made a big difference to us. One evening, at the school, gas masks were distributed to everyone. We had to carry them everywhere. They had adjustable straps with safety pins to fit over your head. I well remember the first air raid we ever had. I was convinced I would be gassed because I had removed the safety pins and nothing held firm.

When Endon School was built we lost all the senior pupils from Bagnall and we were down to three teachers, Effie Stanistreet, Cis Brassington and Charlie Hargreaves.

Then the evacuees came! First from Manchester and later from London. There were a lot more from London, and they were 'streetwise'! The school was now too small to accommodate us, so we had to resort to a shift pattern - mornings and afternoons.

The evacuees also brought some teachers with them. I can recall three. There was one gentleman whose name I cannot remember, Miss Shopland and their headmaster. Everyone called him 'Pop Woller'.

The children gathered on The Green for the Silver Jubilee celebrations for George V and Queen Mary 1935.

The Rev'd. Shone led the service.

The children paraded to The Green for the Silver Jubilee celebrations in 1935.

The Silver Jubilee of George V and Queen Mary.

A Birthday Party group in 1939.
Front row, Left to Right: Audrey Shenton, Valerie Sylvester, June Webb.
2nd row: Dorothy Brown, Marjorie Shenton, Glenis Pegg, Barbara Mayer, Barbara Platt.
3rd row: Betty Allmark, Kathleen Sylvester, Doreen Davies.

He was a tall, thin man with white hair. What I remember most about him was his cane. He always kept it right in front of him on his desk. Charlie Hargreaves had a thick cane, about an inch thick; Pop Woller's was long and thin and very bendy. It must have felt very keen across your hand.

Eventually as time went on we were integrated into one school, and back to normal hours. Another feature about the war years was that Cis Brassington used to teach the girls sewing and knitting. At one time she had us knitting mittens for the wrens. I once received a thank you letter from wren who came from Inverness. She had been the recipient of a pair that I had knitted - it made the effort worthwhile.

Another event at the time was the building of the school air raid shelter. It snaked all over the schoolhouse garden, and inside there were wooden seats on either side. At first we had practice sessions, but eventually they dropped off.

I left Bagnall School in 1943 to go to Westwood Hall Girls' High School in Leek. However I still had associations with the school, as apart from the Church Hall, the school was the only place large enough for social events.

After a while a youth club was formed which met once a week in the school. Cis Brassington and Mrs Brammer took the girls; Albert Wood and Herbert Walsh took the boys. We used to get talks, demonstrations etc. We also held dances most weeks and even formed our own band. Arthur Garner (former London evacuee who stayed here and married Brown Edge girl, Norah Baddeley) played drums. Roy Winkle from the Stafford Arms played the accordion and I played the piano.

My final memories of Bagnall School came in 1959 and 1960 when I took my daughter and then my son to school for their first day, to be taught by the same teacher who first taught me way back in 1937 - Effie Stanistreet."

Alan Beckett:

"I travelled to Bagnall School for the first few weeks with my cousin Joan Millington, and with C.H. Hargreaves, the headmaster, who lived next door to us in Fowler's Lane, Baddeley Edge. He was one of the few people in those days to own a car.

My recollection of Miss Stanistreet's class was a very large room with high windows, and Miss Stanistreet (who appeared quite old to us then) sitting at a table next to a stove pot, which was the heating system for the room. Even in those days everything around the room appeared bright and beautiful. We sat at an old desk and the writing was done on a slate, before we had ink wells with a pen and nib.

The first register I remember was something about 2 feet square and was called in a morning and after lunchtime. I think we had our bottle of milk at breaktime all through the war. We had to recite our tables as a class out aloud - 2x2 are 4, etc. To go to the toilet you had to put your hand up, *"Please Miss, can I leave the room?"* The toilets were outside in the playground, which if I remember had to be emptied regularly.

The school nurse would come around checking your hair, and I vaguely remember the school board man coming to check on any truancy by those not at school. Some lessons in the Summer months were taken in a field belonging to Farmer Clowes - I remember the buttercups and daisies and sitting under a tree having lessons - it was wonderful, and the sun always seemed to shine in Summer when we were young.

I used to catch the bus at Light Oaks at ten to nine, and there was always a push to see who could get the front seat. I was 'made' if the 'flat-fronted' bus arrived and I could sit next to the driver. There would always be a conductor who would click your ticket ($^1/_2$d in old money). His machine made a sort of jingling noise.

Mrs Edge and Miss Edge were the school caretakers who lived in the house in the schoolyard. Mrs Edge looked very old to us, with a long skirt and apron, and her hair in a bun. (I am not sure if she had any teeth in - but you get the picture). She always appeared to be cross with the kids.

The 1940 Winter was a very bad time, with huge snowdrifts through to about March. When the snow first started we were at school. We were sent home early because of the drifting and we walked home through Brown's fields and the golf links, where we were nearly buried in the drifting snow. Embrey's bread van was buried under the snow outside the church.

The evacuees came from London and Manchester. John Stace stayed with Mrs Goodall in the mews cottages below Lord's Farm, and Ronnie Reeves stayed with Miss Edge in the school house, and there were many more. I vividly remember a huge tussle going on between one of the bigger evacuees from London and Mr Hargreaves. He had done something wrong and was holding onto the railings and could not be prised away, but Mr Hargreaves had to win the day for the sake of discipline.

There was a folding partition between Miss Brassington's class and that of Mr Hargreaves. When Miss Brassington had one of her shouting bouts, which was quite often, Mr Hargreaves would cringe on the other side of the partition: a bit like Mainwaring in Dad's army.

One day about half a dozen off us went to Cooper's orchard - at the side of the path leading to the 'Old Mills', scrumping for apples. We had our short trousers tucked into our socks, and they were bulging with apples. Mrs Cooper came to school and we were lined up by Mr Hargreaves and given the cane on both hands.

I took the 11 plus exam in the bottom room, next to Miss Brassington's class - I can't remember this room being used for much else in those days.

After leaving Bagnall school for Leek High School I later went to the youth club on a Friday night. I would go up the 7 o'clock bus, and always when I went into Miss Stanistreet's classroom the record of 12th Street Rap would be playing on the gramophone. Mr Wood took the youth club. He would come on the bus with his bag: a bit like Roy Cropper, but someone with a heart of gold. He would refer to the youth club members as "Youse lads".

I always say that we had wonderful times as children brought up on Baddeley Edge and at Bagnall during the war years, and we were so fortunate living in that area."

The W.I. Christmas Party ? late 1950s. Front row: Mrs Mayer, Barbara Boulton, Jessie Brereton, Greta Booth.
2nd Row includes: Annie Bott, Mrs Hampson.  3rd row includes Annie Bailey, Doris Potts, Evelyn Beckett.

The Bagnall well dressing in 1963. The well at The Springs was decorated by Mr Sargeant.
The pictures were designed by John Hassall and represented Faith, Hope and Charity.

# Chapter 5
# The War Years 1939-45

Dinners were not provided at the school until after the war. Many children travelled home for lunch and then raced back again for afternoon school. However some children had to remain at school as it was too far to return home, so they would bring sandwiches or a potato for their teacher to cook on the stove.

At home each child had a ration book, and the coupons were used for tea, butter, sugar, cheese, meat etc. The rations seemed to be very small. Coupons were needed for sweets and chocolate and they were soon used up. However there was a stall in Hanley Market where people were able to buy some sweets without coupons. Fruit was not very plentiful, as it was difficult for supplies to be shipped in from abroad. It was difficult to buy oranges and the children never saw bananas until after the war. At that time there were long queues to purchase them and many children didn't realise that the skins had to be peeled off before they could be eaten. Apples and pears were available, and sometimes if a child had an apple to eat there would be a queue of children begging for the core. During the Summer months there was rhubarb from the gardens to eat and blackberries could be picked from the hedgerows.

Spoonfuls of orange juice and cod liver oil were handed out at school in an attempt to supplement the diet. Many villagers, in response to the government's urge to 'Dig for Victory', grew their own vegetables wherever they were able. Tomatoes and other fruits were preserved by bottling them, and jams were made when the sugar was available. Eggs were preserved in isinglass. Dried eggs and dried milk could be bought in the shops.

Some mothers even made Easter eggs out of cocoa, condensed milk and dried milk. It was amazing how enterprising they were with these items. There were daily talks on the wireless about imaginative ways to stretch out the food rations, and talks from the family doctor on how to stay fit and healthy. Some fathers would walk over the common or through the fields with their shot guns looking for a tasty rabbit to take home to be made into rabbit stew. A number of people kept chickens and a few kept pigs. A number of neighbours would have a share in a pig and collect their scraps to feed it with. When it was killed they would receive a share of the meat. The killing had to be undertaken by a qualified slaughterer from the Ministry of Food, but a lucrative trade flourished in the 'Black Market' if people had the right contacts.

During the war years the boys wore jackets and short trousers. Some would wear clogs, which would produce sparks when they ran across the schoolyard. Coupons were needed to buy new clothes and they had to stretch a long way, as they were needed for new blankets, bed linen, curtains etc. Mother's dresses were often altered to fit the girls in the family, and clothes had to be passed from one child to another. Every piece of material that was available was used, and clothes were mended and patched and patched again. Even sacking was used for the needlework lessons in the school.

When the children were at school and the air raid sirens were heard they would walk to the school shelter in the caretaker's garden. They would sit round on wooden benches and sing and tell stories to wile away the time until the 'all clear' siren was heard. More often than not the sirens would go off during the early evening or in the middle of the night, when the drone of the German planes going over to bomb Manchester would be heard. They went over night after night. It is believed that they used the reflection from Stanley Pool and Rudyard Lake to assist them in plotting their course. Both adults and children soon learned to identify the sounds of the different aircraft.

Logs and tree trunks were laid across the golf course at Bagnall to prevent enemy planes from landing. The children enjoyed jumping over these on their way home from school. One day a plane crashed on the golf course near the reservoir that used to stand at the top of Bagnall Bank, just by Mrs Dale's cottage. It was a British plane, a Spitfire, and the villagers were distressed to discover later on that the pilot had bailed out, but had died on impact when he landed at Blackshaw Moor. Many locals went to inspect the plane, and one enterprising young man collected up the perspex glass and made jewellery from it to sell to his friends.

The nearest bomb that dropped was by the 'Steps' at Trent Terrace near Abbey Hulton and some houses were destroyed. At night time there were no lights anywhere, so from Light Oaks and Baddeley Edge incendiary bombs could be clearly seen being dropped over the Potteries. Some families in the village hid under their beds, in cellars, or under the stairs, or under tables in the kitchen. Others constructed underground bunkers in their gardens, and lined them with stone, concrete and galvanized iron. At Light Oaks the neighbours gathered in a cellar at the Hurst's home, next door to Mr James' shop (Woodland Stores). They entered through a little door at the side of the house. As the war continued people became more blasé and simply stayed in bed, pulling the bedclothes around their ears. People in the village stuck sticky paper in a grid pattern over their windows to prevent the glass from shattering if a bomb dropped nearby.

A number of men from the village were drafted into the armed forces. Some were in reserved occupations like farming or coal-mining and were exempt. Many of these volunteered for the ARP and spent their evenings patrolling the village. They ensured that the blackout curtains were drawn in the houses, so that no chinks of light could be seen to alert the enemy planes. Some would spend evenings on fire watch at Stoke Church or at the top of other high rise buildings in the city. A number of the women without children were sent to the munitions factory at Swynnerton to work.

Daphne Evans recalls hearing a German plane just skimming her house in School Road and she was so frightened she actually fell into the fire. Afterwards she suffered nightmares in which Germans were attempting to enter her house through the bedroom windows. People had to carry their gas masks wherever they went and Daphne remembers the special gas mask carrycots for the babies. If the children went to school without their gas masks they were sent home to collect them. The air raid siren for Bagnall was located at the hospital and Mr Bowler from School Road left home each evening to help with the night shift there.

Her father joined the Home Guard and was detailed to patrol the golf links armed with one of Farmer Brown's pitch forks in case German paratroopers landed there. He was ordered not to engage them in a fight but to report back to headquarters. Later he was drafted into the army and trained at Shrewsbury Barracks. Daphne travelled with her mother and father on the train to Shrewsbury after a spell of leave. She remembers her parents kiss as they said goodbye, wondering when they would all be together again.

Shortly afterwards Mr Evans was sent to Africa, where he wrote letters back home to the family on stiff creamy coloured paper. He was due to be moved to Burma but fortunately by this time the war was drawing to its close.

Everyone listened to the wireless to hear Churchill's latest speech and to follow the advancing armies. 'Lily of the lamplight', 'It's a long way to Tipperary', 'We'll keep the home fires burning' and 'We'll meet again', echoed throughout the land.

During the war years double Summer time was introduced to help the farmers and it stayed light until really late at night. The children in the village helped with the farm work and with the hay-making. They loved riding to the hay fields in a horse drawn cart.

There was quite a fire in the village when Lord's hay barn next to the cottages on Springs Bank caught fire due to internal combustion. Fortunately it was soon contained and the cottages were undamaged. There were lots of small farms surrounding the village in those days, and the large metal churns were placed outside the farm gates every morning for collection by the dairy lorry. Some milkmen still measured out the milk with ladles into jugs left out on their doorsteps by the villagers.

During the war years the Woman's Institute continued to meet in the village. It had been formed at Bagnall in 1921. Sometimes the ladies met in the Church Hall and later on it is believed they met in Bagnall School. The rules were signed on March 14th 1921 with Mrs M.J. Hassall of Lime Tree Farm as the president, Mrs S. Yarwood from Greenway Hall, Baddeley Edge as the treasurer and Mrs E. Brassington of The Nook, Bagnall as the secretary. Their meetings were held on the second Monday of the month.

The ladies enjoyed talks on various topics, held competitions, organised concerts, produced plays and entered the Leek Show competitions each year - with a lot of success. They supported numerous charities and attended AGMs at the Royal Albert Hall in London.

### Elaine Wood

"I particularly remember Joe coming as an evacuee. He arrived from London with his two brothers who were billeted with Mr and Mrs Potts at Clewlow's Bank, Bagnall. Joe was separated from them and billeted with Miss Woolliscroft in Jack Haye Lane, Light Oaks.

Joe was not happy at being parted from the rest of his family. Miss Woolliscoft was a single lady, living on her own and certainly not used to having a lively 10 year old boy

Bagnall W.I. birthday party in the late 1940s or early 50s.  Some of those on the front row include
Mrs Brayford, Mrs A, Bott, Mrs Bowen and Miss Sherratt
Second row: Dora Sylvester, Mrs Glover, Mrs Thursfield and Mrs Woolley.
Third Row: Mrs Millington, Mrs Eardley, Mrs Allmark.
Fourth row: Mrs Brereton, Mrs N. Beckett and Mrs Sylvester.

Mrs Brereton and her friends enjoying tea and sandwiches at the W.I.

W.I. Birthday Party in the 1960s. Included in the photograph are Mrs Evelyn Beckett, Mrs Bowen, Mrs Hampson, Mrs Kent, Mrs Mayer and Mrs May Eardley.

Some of the evacuees dressed up for a carnival.

Another W.I. Birthday celebration in the 1960s.
This group includes Mrs N. Beckett, Mrs Eardley and Ethel Bailey.

W.I. Bring and Buy sale in the 1960s.

running round the house.  However people coped as best they could in those days.

Joe helped to deliver the newspapers and joined the choir at Bagnall Church.  Mr Bird from The Hollies School in Jack Haye Lane befriended Joe, and made a difference to his stay at Light Oaks.  Eventually Joe returned to London but his two brothers stayed for a while longer.  He has never forgot his stay in the area and he still keeps in contact.

In front of Brown's Farm (Old Hall Farm) was a large pond and we spent many lunchtimes fishing for tadpoles in there.  I remember a village sports day on the green in front of the Farm, and one of the competitions was to catch a live pig that was covered in grease.  It was really difficult to catch and caused much amusement amongst the villagers.

The highlights of school life for me were the nature walks through the Hough Wood and down to The Old Mills. At the Springs the fields were full of celandine and marsh marigolds in the Springtime and we would gather armfuls to put in the glass jars on a table in our classroom.

We did needlework with Miss Brassington. We made draw string bag s out of canvas. I embroidered a pink lotus flower with green leaves on mine, and I was really proud of it.

During the war when I attended Endon School, the Headmaster, Mr. Ingley, was keen to train the children to help with casualties and rescue work.  My friend and I had to wait outside James' shop at Light Oaks to be collected by an ambulance. We were then put on stretchers and driven to Endon School where we were put into beds - stored under the stage in the school hall - and our injuries treated by the first aid team."

## Margaret Walley

"My name was Margaret Colley then and during the war years I lived at Stanley Farm. We had quite a bit of accommodation in the farmhouse and so we were allocated some evacuees. The first to arrive were a group of children from Manchester. I remember they refused to drink any milk when they realised that it came from a cow.

They were quite a rough bunch, but their mother came to visit them every Sunday to see how they were coping with life in the country.  I remember my mother being quite annoyed because she always insisted on sitting with the children in our front room which was very special to us. However, after a short time they decided to move on.

Then, quite a well off couple arrived with their two children, a nurse and two dogs. They were the Samuel family and they came from London.  They had been staying at the Ash Bank Hotel, but the Ministry had taken it over and they had to leave. Mr Samuel was in the RAF and was working with the Air Ministry at Kingsley Holt.  The toddler was aged three and the little one was six months.

The nurse stayed with us for about a year and seemed to enjoy caring for the children. She left for some reason and another girl arrived to care for the children.  This girl was called Rose and said she was eighteen and had quite a bit of experience with little ones. When she had been with us for about five months I realised that whilst I had been doing the washing two of our pillow cases had gone missing.  This really puzzled me, until one day after Rose had been doing some of the children's washing and left it in a wet pile, I decided to hang it up on the rack to dry for her. I was amazed to find amongst the pile two vests that had been made from our pillow cases. She denied that she had used our pillow cases and insisted that she had brought them with her.

Then one day there was a knock at our door and two policemen were standing there. They asked lots of questions about the Rose. Apparently she had taken the children for a walk from Stanley to Stockton Brook one day when a bus had arrived from Hanley and her brother and mother were on it. It turned out they had been searching for her, because she had run away from home and she was only fourteen. But Mrs Samuel asked if Rose could remain with us at the farm and her family agreed to the arrangement.

The Samuel family left us before the end of the war and the Rev. Johnson and his wife were billeted with us. They were originally from Bootle and had been staying at a farm at Leek. Mrs Johnson was a doctor. The Rev. Johnson taught English at Leek High School as well as working as a minister. One day he asked if he could store some furniture with us and we agreed to it. In due course some rather nice pieces of furniture arrived. They had arranged for some other furniture to be stored in various places in the Leek area. One day we noticed two men walking past the farmhouse. They were plain clothes policemen. Apparently the Johnson's were attempting to claim quite a lot of money from insurance companies for this furniture, claiming that it had been destroyed or had gone missing.

Yes, the war years were interesting times for us, and even more interesting were the evacuees. The evacuees arrived in Bagnall be coach and they were taken into the school. The families who had been allocated evacuees had to select the children they thought would fit into their family best. The evacuees were nice children, but some had come from poor homes and had to be kitted out with clothes."

Daphne Evans recalls some evacuees living with them in School Road. They had some older children from Liverpool billeted with them and then a couple from London came. The man did not want to return to London and he was so distressed that one day he went to the top of the Hough Wood Lane and tried to shoot himself. Daphne's mother heard the shot and ran to investigate. She calmed him down and took him home for some medical treatment, but the authorities removed him from Bagnall, as they considered him to be too dangerous to have in the village. At one point there were thirteen people living in Mrs Evans' house because other relations were there as well as the family and the evacuees.

After the war was over in 1945 there were great celebrations. In many parts of the country street parties were held, the streets decorated with bunting. Long tables stretched along the streets, and were laden with sandwiches, cakes and jellies of all varieties. At Bagnall, flags were put out, a party was held in the school and a bonfire lit on the Green.

At Light Oaks a grand carnival was held in the field behind the Baptist Chapel. It was hoped that the money raised would go towards building a village hall for the Bagnall, Light Oaks and Baddeley Edge area. Valerie Sylvester (now Whittaker) was crowned queen, and Audrey Shenton (now Rennie) was also a queen. The children from Bagnall School and other schools in the area were in the retinues.

Rehearsals were held in a large garage at the side of Shenton's house in Light Oaks Avenue. After the crowning ceremony the crowds were entertained with a fancy dress parade for adults and children and maypole dancing. The children used half hoops covered with fresh flowers to perform one of their dance displays to the music of 'The Skaters Waltz'. Some of the girls had their hair specially curled with ringlets, produced by taking bunches of hair and winding strips of cloth around, tied at the bottom, and then the girls slept with them in place. When the rags were removed the following morning, their hair was a mass of ringlets.

To celebrate the end of the war, a canal boat trip was organised at Stockton Brook. The families from Bagnall and Light Oaks walked over the fields and the golf course to Stockton Brook, and climbed onto a barge that was waiting for them. It was the first time many of the children had been on a boat trip. They were fascinated when they arrived at the locks and felt the boat getting lower and lower as the lock water emptied, as they gazed up at the dripping wet slimy walls in disbelief.

Other annual carnivals followed at Light Oaks. These were held in the field on the other side of the road from the Baptist Chapel. Again the Bagnall schoolchildren were in the retinues and joined in the dancing. The dancing troupe was known at 'The Baddeley Edge Bluebells'. One year Christine Platt from Yew Tree was crowned as the queen. She drank water from the well at Spout Lane, Baddeley Edge, and the Rev. Sanderson from St. Chad's conducted a ceremony there.

From the 1920s the crowning of the Rose Queen had been a tradition at Bagnall. Hannah Brown, Rose Edge and Dorothy Potts were some of the queens. During the war years these ceremonies were discontinued, but after the Light Oaks celebrations the Rose Queen crowning ceremonies at Bagnall were re-established in 1952, when Ann Bosson from Rockfield Avenue, Light Oaks was crowned. These ceremonies were organised by the Church. For many many years Mrs Elsie Smith from Milton helped to train the children. The ceremony took place in Mr Lord's field to the rear of the Church Hall and there were stalls and games for the villagers. There were donkey rides, tugs of war and bowling for a side of ham.

In 1956 when Jennifer Edge was crowned queen, the Countess of Shrewsbury came along to perform the crowning ceremony. She looked very glamorous in her Dior dress and large hat. The band played and the Scottish dancers and Maypole dancers entertained the crowds. Refreshments were served in the Church Hall.

In 1963, in Rev. David Price's time at curate at St. Chad's, there was a piano smashing competition in the quarry at the top of Mill Lane - some of the villagers didn't approve of this event. The ceremony disappeared for a time but in 1997 they were revived by the villagers and Capt. Frank McGregor from St Chad's, to celebrate the 100th anniversary of the planting of the Chestnut trees on the Green for Queen Victoria's Diamond Jubilee. The title Rose Queen was changed to Chestnut Queen.

Valerie Sylvester was the Baddeley Edge/Light Oaks Carnival Queen.
L to R: June Eardley, Sheila Deaville, June Ball, Marilyn Minett, Valerie Sylvester,
Josephine Beckett, Maureen Ball, Peter Beckett.

Christine Platt and Pat Bevington with their retinues at the well in Spout Lane, Baddeley Edge.
L to R: Maureen Ball, Christine Platt, Pat Bevington, June Ball, Rev Sanderson, Janet Bainbridge, Sheila Deaville

The fancy dress competition at the Light Oaks Carnival was very popular. Left: Mrs Malkin, Jessie Brereton, Mrs Downes, Greta Booth, Honor Bainbridge, Edith Deaville

Dorothy Potts was the Bagnall Queen in the 1920s

Vera Forrester was the Bagnall Rose Queen in 1927

Anne Bosson was the Rose Queen in 1952 when the crowning ceremony was revived at Bagnall.

In 1956 Jennifer Edge was crowned as the Bagnall Queen by the Countess of Shrewsbury. Margaret Sheldon is the queen (on the left). Gordon Williams was the curate at that time, and standing near to him is the rector's wife Mrs Pearce. Percy Bailey can be seen in the background.

Helping at one of the Garden Fetes in the 1950s were Marion Ford, Joyce Rowley and Margaret Corbishley.

Ann Brayford 1960.

Sheila Glover was crowned in 1962. The Rev'd Kenneth Broadhurst and his wife Shirley are on the left

Rebecca Whieldon was crowned in 1972.

A gathering of the Queens in 1965. The Rev'd. David Price is on the back row.

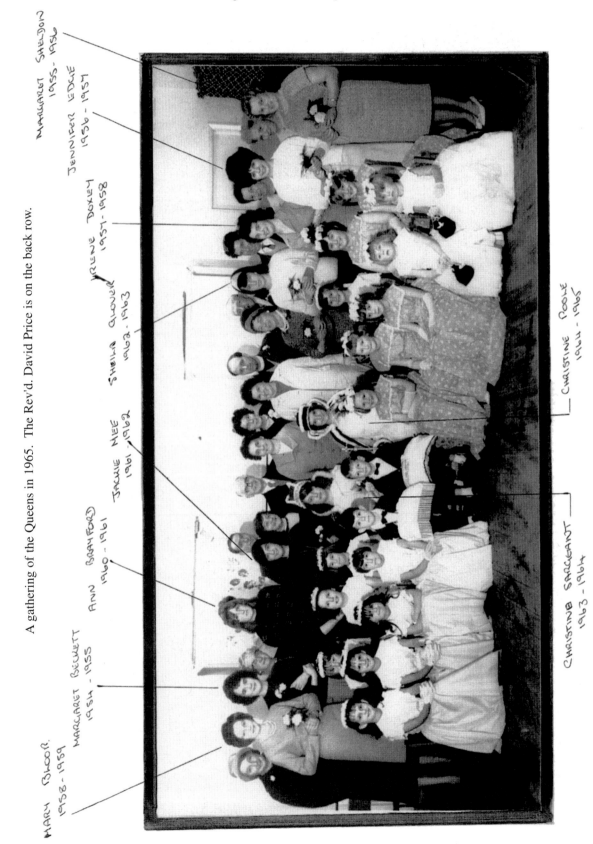

MARGARET SHELDON 1955 - 1956

JENNIFER LEDGE 1956 - 1957

IRENE DOXEY 1957 - 1958

SHEILA GLOVER 1962 - 1963

JACKIE MEE 1961 - 1962

ANN BRAYFORD 1960 - 1961

MARGARET BECKETT 1954 - 1955

MARY BLOOR 1958 - 1959

CHRISTINE POOLE 1964 - 1965

CHRISTINE SARGEANT 1963 - 1964

Margaret Wallett and Janet Bainbridge serving drinks.

Country Dancing in the 1960s.

Country Dancing in the 1960s.

.Josephine Hedley was the Rose Queen in 1960.

Presentations to the Youth Club members.

Bagnall Youth Club football team about 1946.  Back row: Ivan Jackson, Trevor Radcliff, Gordon Simpson. Seated: Donald Eardley, Barry Cooper, Albert Wood (Youth Club Leader), Phil Griffiths (Coach), Michael Johnson, Howard Brown. Front row: Jones and John Boulton.

A Youth Club Party.

# Chapter 6
# The Youth Club

Elaine Wood:

"During the war years we girls used to meet at Miss Brassington's house one week, and at Mrs Brammer's on Clewlow's Bank the next, to do craft work. We used to make flowers from wax and do cork wool. To do the cork wool we had a wooden cotton reel with four little nails in the top and the wool was wound round the nails. You had to keep pulling the loops of wool over to produce the knitting.

At the end of the war two lads, Joe Wain and Clive Mountford, came to visit my father, Councillor Albert Wood, to see if there was a possibility of starting a youth club in the village. My father was serving on the Parish Council and Leek Rural District Council, and they felt he might be able to influence the necessary people - and my father succeeded in booking Bagnall School on Tuesday evenings to hold the youth club meetings there.

At first the club was unaffiliated and just catered for the boys. Then other volunteers agreed to help. Mr Bird from The Hollies School, and Doug Brayford and Herbert Walsh were very enthusiastic. Then Phil Griffiths, a Welsh International football player, agreed to coach the boys for football and other sports. The Rev. Sanderson from St. Chad's offered to help too. Eventually it became officially affiliated to Staffs County Council Youth Clubs and then everything had to done to the letter. They had blue and white badges to wear, and the motto was 'Service not self'.

As travel became easier, they decided to visit Great Yarmouth to camp under canvas, a great adventure for the boys. My father hired a lorry and they set off with him driving and my mother in the front seat, and all the boys and equipment in the back. Rationing continued for a while after the war, but Youth Clubs were allocated extra points so they took provisions with them, including bread, tea, sugar, lard, flour, butter, tins of salmon and spam - and a butcher in Great Yarmouth supplied them with meat. I remembered my father saying that there were several loaves of bread in the back of the lorry - then someone sat on them!

In later years they visited Weymouth and Paignton, Great Yarmouth for a second time, and then Hastings a number of times. Instead of the lorry they opted for the comfort of the trains. In Hastings one year one of the Wain boys was rushed to hospital with appendicitis. In Weymouth they experienced the luxury of being billeted in huts and even had a tuck shop.

One year some German ships were anchored in the harbour dressed overall with bunting and flags and some of the bunting went missing. Suspicions fell upon the Bagnall boys, but when enquiries were made, Mr Bird assured the authorities that the boys would never dream of committing such a crime!

Eventually in the 1950s the girls joined the club on Friday evenings, when there was dancing to the gramophone. Mr Joe Pratt and Mrs Edith Deaville from Light Oaks led the dancing and taught the youngsters to waltz, and quick-step to the music of Glen Miller and other famous bands. These Friday evening sessions in Miss Stanistreet's classroom were a great success. In some ways it seemed a little unfair as the tutors taking the classes or doing the sports coaching were paid for their work, but my father as the Youth Club leader received nothing. But he did

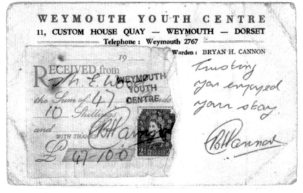

it because he had the interest of the youngsters at heart, and wanted to do his best for them.

My father arranged outings and day trips. He took parties of youngsters to the Youth Services at Lichfield Cathedral and for many of them it was the first time they had ever visited Lichfield. He organised visits to other youth clubs in Walsall and other parts of Staffordshire. The football team joined the league and played matches in a field at the top of Old Mills Lane. It wasn't in the best of condition but the boys turned up faithfully week after week, often playing in appalling conditions - and of course there were no showers for them to use afterwards.

Membership of the club was not restricted to Bagnall and Light Oaks, boys came from Norton, Abbey Hulton, Endon, Baddeley Green and Milton to the Tuesday evening meetings. Mr Bird taught at Bradeley and he encouraged boys from his school to join, often paying for them to go to camp himself. Other people became involved with the club: Tony Asplin, Maurice Johnson and Bert Frost contributed a great deal to the running of the group.

Sadly, my father died in 1960, after devoting fifteen years to the running of the club. So many youngsters were grateful to him for his foresight in starting the club and for his determination and enthusiasm to make it succeed which brought adventure and fun to their lives. After his death he was succeeded by Mr Bailey and Mr Myatt."

Terry Chetwin:

"When I was a youngster we lived at Milton and the family moved from what was known as 'bottom Milton' to 'top Milton'. At that time I was singing in the choir at Norton Church and I used to enjoy playing jokes on my fellow choristers. One day I took a bunch of spring onions from home and proceeded to eat them during the service, much to the disgust of the rest of the choir. After the service the Rev Mackenzie caught me in the vestry and wanted to know what I had been doing. I explained and was instantly dismissed from the choir.

Mrs Elsie Smith heard of my plight and invited me to join the choir at St. Chad's, Bagnall. And in due course became involved with the Youth Club at the school and the irrepressible Captain Wood. My time at the Youth Club changed my life for ever.

On Tuesday evenings we enjoyed P.T. with Phil Griffiths, an ex Port Vale player. Of course we boys idolised him and regarded him as our role model.

A presentation to David Gibson.
Front row: Kay Holdcroft, Joe Pratt, Margaret Wallet, David Gibson, Mrs Wood, Albert Wood (Youth Club
Leader), Frank Bird, Annie Mountford, Sheila Deaville, Janet Bainbridge.
Back row includes:  Bob Hassall, Terry Chetwin, Elaine Wood,  and Doug Holdcroft.

Bagnall Youth Club Football Team in the 1950s.

On Friday evenings the girls joined us for dancing under the leadership of Joe Pratt and Edith Deaville. At Milton the boys and girls never mixed and it was amazing that at Bagnall they actually danced with each other. We learned all the latest dances - even the square tango, and at the Christmas parties the 'Paul Jones' was great fun.

In 1954 when I was sixteen we went with Captain Wood, Mr Bird and some others to Hastings. We lads sat in the back of an open lorry to Stoke Station and caught a train that took us straight through to Hastings. The whole trip was remarkable value at £14 for the fortnight. There were 40 of us altogether and it was the first time many of us had ever been away from home without our families. It was a wonderful adventure for us - most of the lads had never even seen the sea before. We stayed on the East Hill in huts and the conditions were a bit primitive, but we thought it was terrific.

We took it in turns to help with the chores. During the daytime we went swimming and explored the beach area. During the evenings we visited the town. We never got into any sort of trouble. There were no broken windows, although we did buy cider at 9d a pint. We used to add orange juice to it because it was so bitter. We frequented a café with slot machines which was run by a lovely Greek couple. I will always remember Slim Whitman singing 'Rosemarie' on the jukebox. I think we almost wore the record out. Sometimes we spent an enjoyable evening at the dances on the pier

Graham Evans, one of our lads, forgot to remove his glasses when he dived into the sea one day. Of course he lost them - we searched for them in vain. The lens were really thick, like bottle glass. Eventually we decided we had better take him to an optician in the town to see if he could help. We had to lead him all the way. The optician took him into his little back room and was able to fix him up with some national health glasses. I can still hear him saying, *"There is no way this lad is going out of here without some glasses"*.

By the end of the second week our funds were running low. We often went to Zac's café where we had beefburgers or pie with chips and coffee for 2/6. Alan Lake was with us and because we hadn't got enough money for everything Alan offered to sing for his supper. The owner agreed and Alan stood up and sang 'Come back to Sorrento' in fluent Italian. We were all amazed as we had never heard anything like it, and Alan had his supper free of charge. Alan went on to join the Milton amateur dramatic group, 'The Good Companions' and later trained at RADA. He became a well-known actor and appeared on the television (and famously married Diana Dors!)

As I have said Bagnall Youth Club opened a new way of life to me. In later years I served with the army in Berlin, at the time the wall was being constructed and I witnessed some terrible atrocities as people tried to escape across it. Sometimes I looked back and thought of the happy times we had with Captain Wood, his family, Mr Bird and a lorry full of lads setting off for an adventure in Hastings.

Brian Lewis:

To me Bagnall School meant the twice weekly Youth Club, with Tuesday as training night and Friday as dancing night. I lived in Baddeley Green and got to Bagnall in one of three ways: in the winter I would walk to Milton and catch the Milton Service bus; in the summer I would ride my bike all the way, or I would walk up to the golf course and through the Hough Wood.

Tuesday's meetings were very much a boys' scene with Mr Wood and Phil Griffiths in charge. Phil came to the club with his footballs to encourage boys to take part in physical activity. After an hour of football training we enjoyed table tennis and darts. More boys were attracted to the club and our numbers grew.

With the encouragement given to me by the two Youth Club leaders, in the Autumn of 1953 I went for a trial for the England Youth Club's Rugby team. I was chosen for the open side wing forward position. In the season 1953/4 I played against Wales in Neath and Bristol, and in the following season the opposition was Wales again at Neath and Leicester. My exploits on the international rugby field were highlighted in the 'Evening Sentinel' with Bagnall Youth Club also receiving some due recognition.

Friday's dancing always started with an hour or so of country dancing and ballroom dancing. This was not to every members' liking, but it did get everyone on their feet and mixing with the opposite sex. Here I learned the 'Dashing White Sergeant', the 'Cumberland Square Eight' and many others. I never did manage the 'Polyglide' as the foot movements always defeated me. The only two modern dances that I ever mastered, the waltz and samba, served me well in later life. Following this formal part of the evening, dancing was to the latest hit records with the smooch and jive very popular.

The popularity of these dance sessions was in large part due to the two instructors Mr. Joe Pratt and Mrs. Edith Deaville. They were wonderful dancers and they brought to the schoolroom and elegance and delight that enthused many of the youth club members - who otherwise would never admit their interest or feelings.

The activities of the youth club were not confined to the school rooms, as each year there was Youth Club Service in Lichfield Cathedral and visits to other clubs. The service in the Cathedral was always well attended by youth clubs from all over the county. From Bagnall there was always a full coach of well dressed club members.

A visit to a club in Walsall, probably in late Autumn of 1954, made many members realise how lucky they were to have such a pleasant rural venue for our club. The Walsall club was in run down urban area and most of its members were working - the majority of our members were still at school.

Members of the club gained much from their participation in the many activities. We had a chance to socialise, to develop friendships, to enjoy new sports and dances. We grew up in a protective and stimulating environment. Many past members of the club will, I am certain, have in their possession the youth badge, a shield shape, coloured in blue, white and silver with the County knot and the motto 'Service Not Self'. The sight of this momento will bring back many pleasant memories to many as it does to me.

Bagnall School photograph taken in 1949. Mrs Edge and her daughter Annie are on the left and Miss Stanistreet, Miss Shenton (Oakden), Mrs Billington (Headmistress) are on the right..

# Chapter 7
# Two Teachers
# Miss Effie Stanistreet and Miss Cissie Brassington

Miss Effie Stanistreet had started her teaching career at the school as a pupil teacher in 1920, the same year that Mr Hargreaves took up the post of headteacher. She completed 42 years in the school retiring in 1962.

In 1939 when the senior pupils transferred to Endon she moved with the infants from the small overcrowded room to Class 1. The gallery had been removed and it was a large airy room with light streaming in from a number of large windows.

At dinnertime those children who could return home for a meal were duly dispatched. The children who stayed used the large old stove to cook the potatoes they had brought along with them. The days of the provision of dinners by the school had not yet arrived. Directly in front of the stove, where she could enjoy the heat from the fire, she placed her desk.

On the wall at the side of the desk were two honours boards inscribed with the names of the children who had gained scholarships to the local grammar schools. The list appeared to be discontinued after 1930. The walls were tiled half way up, the floor was composed of beautiful oak parquet blocks which were sprinkled with sparkly flakes when dances were to be held in the room. Some of those children remember sliding over the flake covered blocks to make them really slippy for the dancing. The window sills were always full of geraniums, giving a warm glow to the room.

When the Infants initially arrived at the age of 4 or 5 their first task was to copy numbers from the blackboard.

A favourite occupation enjoyed by the Infants was threading coloured beads onto shoe laces. The colours of the beads were thrilling, but it is a wonder the beads weren't swallowed by mistake. The children practiced their reading and writing skills, and there

Number work in the Infant class.

were stories and poems to enjoy.  Miss Stanistreet played the piano and the songs echoed throughout the school: 'Ferry me across the water, do boatman do, If you've a penny in your purse, I'll ferry you'; at Harvest time 'We plough the fields and scatter' played with great vigour; and at Christmas the little ones would sweetly sing 'Away in a manger'.

Life wasn't always easy for all the little ones in the Infant's class.  One former pupil remembers arriving at the school after Christmas.  She was just aged five but was caned for not being able to read the book that was put in front of her.  This only stopped when the parents complained and considered moving her to another school.  However the lost time was made up for when the child was taught to read by her Aunt during the Easter holidays.

Joyce Rowley:

"I was only four when I started school at Bagnall and I was with Miss Stanistreet in the big classroom.  Mr Hargreaves was with the class next door, Miss Brassington was in Class 3 and at that time Miss Mathers was in the little room at the end.

I remember the big stove where Miss Stanistreet stood to keep warm.  I spent my time working with plasticine, doing number work and listening to stories.  I remember copying a poem about a robin.  Miss Stanistreet was very kind and would sometimes give me gifts especially at Christmas time - I was delighted to receive a little bottle of perfume one year.

The boys moved the milk crates with the little bottles of milk we had to drink each day.  I used to travel to school on the bus, and we purchased our little book of halfpenny tickets each week.  There were no school dinners in those days, so I had to travel home at dinner time and then rush to catch the bus back again, all within the hour.

When I was just about to transfer to Miss Brassington's class I had rheumatic fever and was at home for quite a time.

In Miss Brassington's class I did a lot of knitting.  As it was wartime I used to knit mittens and socks for the men and women serving in the forces.  I had help with the difficult parts and I was delighted when the school received a letter thanking us for our efforts.

Miss Leese taught at the school at one time.  She lived at Bradshaw Farm along Baddeley Edge and she helped to take the Sunday School classes at the Methodist Chapel. She was really nice and everyone was pleased when she married Mr Shone, the curate at the St. Chad's Church.

When the evacuees came we were so overcrowded we just had to attend school for half a day.  We attended in the mornings and when we went home the remaining children went in for the afternoon session.

At one time the Bagnall Sunday School was so large the Sunday School children could not be accommodated in the Sunday School building and permission had to be sought for some of them to meet in the school each Sunday.

The school was also used for a youth club.  Miss Brassington and Mrs Brammer helped with this to begin with.  Mr Wood from Light Oaks worked hard for the youth club and later Mr Pratt taught ballroom dancing with the help of Mrs Deaville.

I left Bagnall School to attend senior school at Endon when I was 10, but after a year I transferred to Leek, Westwood Hall Girls' High school."

Daphne Evans

"I have vivid memories of my first day at Bagnall School. I remember wearing a dark brown coat and leggings with lots of buttons at the side and a little bonnet. In the cloakroom I was helped out of my clothes by one of the teachers. The clothes pegs were too high for me to hang my things so I had to be helped.

There was a small tear in the lining of my coat - I was very upset when the person helping me remarked, *"Fancy sending a child to school in a ripped coat!"* My mother had been so busy looking after all the people living at home that she hadn't had time to see to the problem, but I felt ashamed by this careless remark for a long time afterwards.

Miss Stanistreet's room had a large stove in it with iron railings around and her desk was right in front of it. We had slates to write on and we used to chant as we worked - *"b flies through this window, and d flies through that window."* We had to point to the appropriate windows with our arms as we chanted. Then we had to do rows of b's and d's on our slates.

I loved some of the activities in her class. We would have tins full of coloured beads and strings and we would thread the beads on to the strings for what seemed like hours and hours. At Christmas time we would be given crepe paper that Miss Stanistreet had cut out to look like orchid petals. We had to ruche them up along a needle. She then threaded the flowers through strings and suspended them from P.T. hoops from the ceiling.

At Christmas we would have fancy dress competitions and I remember one year Malcolm Potts won the first prize for the boys dressed up to represent Robin Hood. I won the first prize for the girls as Alice Blue Gown. I wore a beautiful pale blue muslin dress with pink plastic roses round the collar, and sandals on my feet that I could hardly walk in. I walked around the room singing 'In my Alice Blue Gown....'. The prize was a little bit disappointing. Miss Stanistreet had made it and it consisted of a bracelet made out of sheering elastic with green and white buttons threaded onto it.

I loved the music lessons at school, I remember 'See the little catkins cover all the slender willows over'. The smell of geraniums pervaded the school. I was a really a good reader and I was sent to Mrs Billington's class to read with the older children.

While I was in Miss Stanistreet's class I saw my brother Ken in one of the plays. Ken Simpson was also in the play. There was the turret of a large castle and my brother had to gallop up to it on a pretend horse and climb the steps of the castle to rescue the princess imprisoned at the top. Ken wore my father's African bush hat and I really believed that he was climbing the steps of the castle. I felt so proud of him.

In the 1940s Miss Cissie Brassington lived in the semi detached house next door but one to the school, in School Road. She was very strict, but many pupils agreed that she was a good teacher. When the seven year olds entered her classroom they were given slates and pieces of charcoal to write with. At playtime a monitor had the privileged task of wiping the slates clean with a jar of water and a little mop.

The row of cupboards on the opposite wall to the partition was always covered with bright pictures. A favourite set portrayed the poem, 'The Months' by Sara Coleridge.

*January brings the snow, makes our feet and fingers glow,*
*February brings the rain, thaws the frozen lake again,*
*March brings breezes loud and shrill to stir the dancing daffodil,*
*April brings the primrose sweet, scatters daisies at our feet.*
*May brings flocks of pretty lambs, skipping by their fleecy dams.*
*June brings tulips, lilies, roses, fills the children's hands with posies.*
*Hot July brings cooling showers, apricots and gillyflowers.*
*August brings, the sheaves of corn, then the harvest home is bourne.*
*Warm September brings the fruit, sportsmen then begin to shoot.*
*Fresh October brings the pheasant, then to gather nuts is pleasant.*
*Dull November brings the blast, then the leaves are whirling fast.*
*Chill December brings the sleet, blazing fire and Christmas treat.*

Miss Brassington's forte was needlework and crafts. The younger children would weave brightly coloured wools over cardboard frames eventually hoping to turn their efforts into kettle holders. There were not so many electric kettles then and often kettles were boiled on the open fire. As they progressed the girls would make tea cosies embroidered with crinoline ladies surrounded by hollyhocks. However needlework materials were always in short supply and sometimes old sacking would be used to work on. At Christmas time approached the children loved making Christmas cards and calendars made from cardboard covered with wallpaper, with a picture on the front and little calendars glued to the bottom.

Sometimes during the Summer months Miss Brassington would lead her little flock down to the Old Mills and the children would sit in one of the fields whilst she read stories to them. At this time the children were encouraged to save money and little savings books were issued in which they could stick the saving stamps they purchased from school each week for 6d or 2/6. When enough stamps had been saved these could be exchanged for a savings certificate."

Kathleen Harper (Beckett):

"Thinking back to my days at Bagnall School evokes many memories. Being there during the war years meant gas masks and frequent trips to the air raid shelter although I don't think we were even in imminent danger from enemy aircraft.

Sunny days and nature walks to the Houghwood are some of the things I remember about being in Miss Stanistreet's class, also in the run up to Christmas the classroom awash with coloured paper and glue as the annual paper chain and lantern making got underway.

Making the small individual chains was relatively easy, the difficult part was joining them together.

Being in Miss Brassington's class conjures up quite a different picture. I found her quite intimidating at times. I particularly recall the sewing lessons. I did make a rather nice patchwork cushion cover, but had less success with my apron, which I made from one of my Dad's old shirts (material was hard to come by as everything was rationed). Miss Brassington was well known for her cane. I'm pleased to say I was never on the receiving end of any punishment whilst in her class.

Mrs Billington did once rap my knuckles for talking during prayers, but my abiding memory off her was seeing her wash pupils' mouths out with soap if they used what she considered to be bad language. By far the worst memory I have of my time at Bagnall School was the visit from the dentist. I dreaded the time the classroom door opened and my name was called, the fact the nurse commented on my lovely red hair ribbon did nothing to quell my fears.

Mr Hargreaves was noted for his strong discipline and use of the cane to enforce it. Ken Evans remembers when he and his friends were caned for throwing a dead crow around the schoolyard. Corporal punishment was the norm in those days. In 1944 Charlie Hargreaves retired from the headship and Beatrice Billington from Leek was appointed as the new head. Mrs Billington had some previous experience at the school for in one of her letters she stated that she had worked at the school in 1902 as a pupil teacher.

She had a difficult journey each day to get to Bagnall from Nab Hill Avenue in Leek. First of all she had to walk from home to the main Leek to Newcastle Road to catch a P.M.T. bus to Stockton Brook. Then she walked over the bridge on the Stanley road to a track not far from Greenway Hall Golf Club, which climbed up the hillside through the Houghwood to Bagnall. On the way she collected one of the pupils, Helen Berrisford, from one of the lonely cottages on the track and took her along to school. The children from the school would try to meet Mrs Billington when they were able and help her to carry her bags.

Mrs Billington was in her late fifties when she was appointed. She wasn't very tall, and had a mass of short white hair. She often attended school dressed in her green WVS suit and matching hat ready for one of her meetings in the evening when she returned home from school. She beguiled the pupils with stories of her daughter Jean, who had the distinction of swimming the width of Rudyard Lake.

During Mrs Billington's time hot meals were served at lunchtime for the first time. Miss Stanistreet's old classroom was now the new dining room and the meals were brought in containers from Greenways School at Baddeley Green. The tin containers gave the meals a distinct flavour of their own. The meals were served out, with great aplomb, by the caretaker Mrs Edge, and her daughter Annie. Before long Mrs Haywood, from Light Oaks Avenue, came along to help. To begin with the cost for the week's dinners was 2/1d or 5d a day. Later the cost rose to 2/6d.

In those days there was no telephone in the school and no secretarial help. The curriculum concentrated on the three R's: Reading, wRiting and aRithmetic. The mornings were spent working on arithmetic and Mrs Billington always marked the sums if they were correct in her own distinctive way. The afternoons were devoted to story writing, grammar and literature. Some of the books Mrs Billington read out aloud were 'Black Beauty' by Anna Sewell and 'Treasure Island' by R.L. Stevenson. The afternoon usually ended with the children chanting some of the poems they had learned by heart: 'The Lone Dog', 'The Pedlar's Caravan' and 'Meg Merrilees' were some favourites. Basically, the curriculum consisted of Maths, English, a little music, art for the boys, and needlework for the girls. There was no History, Geography or Science and very little P.E. Occasionally they would do music and movement listening to the radio.

Once there was a sports day held on the piece of land at the entrance to the village from the hospital end. The slow bicycle race was one of the highlights.

Christmas time was very special in Mrs Billington's classroom as the children were encouraged to wrap up little gifts for each other and store them ready for Christmas in one of the cupboards. There was great excitement when the day to distribute the presents arrived, and every child appeared to receive lots of toys and books of every type. It didn't matter that they were second-hand and some were wrapped in newspaper. They were just as precious to each recipient as any expensive gifts. The average wage was about £3 a week at the time. There would be parties and a Christmas tree. The classrooms were festooned with decorations of every variety, and the children made the most of the festive season.

At this time the girls developed a passion for bringing round tins of Johnson's furniture polish to school and polishing their desks until they looked like skating rinks. Mrs Billington praised their efforts, but the pervading smell in the classroom was polish."

However all was not well and in 1950 Mrs Billington reported to the school managers that there were problems with the cesspit, and she was also very concerned about some damage that had happened at the youth club. She requested that a billiard table that was unsafe should be removed from the classroom used by the youth club.

Mrs Billington's Report to the Managers, April 5th 1950:
*The Youth club use the Infant's room for football practice and during last term we have been unfortunate in having a pane in a cupboard broken, a door riddled with dart holes and a picture broken down. Two bulbs and a globe have been broken and there is a crack in the clock face. Although only bladders are used, it does not seem to be a suitable place for football practice.*

Sheila Woodward (Deaville):
"I remember a stone building with windows high up so that I could only see the sky. There were three classrooms holding approximately 30 children in each. There was a separate cloakroom for each class. The school was heated by a boiler in the cellar. Only in the Infant's classroom was there a stove with opening doors to let out the heat.

The 'thunderbox' toilets were outside in the yard. The headteacher was Mrs Billington who travelled in each day from Leek. She used the bus to Stockton Brook and walked the rest of the way. Miss Brassington took the next class, and nobody stepped out of line in her class - if they did, it was the slipper, or worse, the split cane. Miss Stanistreet looked after the Infants and was kindly, but firm. There were no classroom assistants in those days. Something must have been right, measured by the number of children who went on to High School and College or University."

Daphne Evans:

"Mrs Billington was fat and matronly. During our Geography lessons she would read to us from Air Mail letters that had been sent to her from her niece in Karachi, and I remember thinking - so this is Geography!

I was thrilled when during the Summer months, when the sun was shining, she took us to the seat on the grass opposite the cottages on Springs Bank and read to us 'The Boy in the Rabbit Skin Cap'. I loved it when we listened to the story - I felt blissfully happy. Later on when I visited Much Wenlock in Shropshire I became friendly with some of the neighbours. The head of the household was a gamekeeper and I could hardly believe it when I discovered that he possessed a copy of 'The Boy in the Rabbit Skin Hat'.

During the fine Summer weather we would push our double desks through the door and out into the school yard and work there out in the sunshine. At the end of the school day we would push the desks into the bike shed for the night, hoping that the following day would be sunny too.

I have vivid memories of bluebells in glass jars and hyacinth bulbs growing in glass bottles until they died and stood in brown dingy water - I always remember thinking they would look much nicer in clean fresh water. In the Spring the classroom would be decorated with pots of hawthorn blossom.

I remember the school dinners and the strange smell that enveloped them. Annie Edge would serve them out and I will never forget the chocolate crunch with pink custard.

The dentist would come to visit us at school and I recall having a tooth removed by a fat musical dentist who kept singing 'Red sails in the sunset' to me as he pulled at the tooth.

In Mrs Billington's class we always said The Lord's Prayer at the beginning of the day and I always thought 'hallowed' was a funny surname to have. At the end of the day we would sing 'Lord keep us safe this night, Secure from all our fears, May angels keep us safe this night, Till morning light appears'. In fact I still sing this every night.

The general atmosphere in the school must have been very quiet compared to classrooms these days because I remember listening for the first mowing machines of the Summer to start work in the fields outside. In those days the mowing machines were pulled by horses and I remember the tick, tick, ticking noises they made. I recall that when the last of the harvest was collected in and we celebrated the harvest home I was allowed to ride one of the horses back to Brown's farm. The horses would wear their brasses to celebrate the harvest home and sometimes the ribbons were taken off my plaits and my hair was woven in with the horse's hair.  Once a fire started where the horses were kept at the farm and we had to run to Clowes's farm to use the telephone to call for help.  There were very few telephones in the village then.

In 1947 the village was cut off by terrific snow storms.  The school was closed for some considerable time.  My brother Ken and his friend Ken Garrett had to sledge to Milton to get some bread for us.  There were tremendous drifts on Clewlow's Bank and we spent halcyon days sledging down the fields at the back of the post office.  There was a huge rock there and when our sledges went over it we were suspended in the air for ages.

One Summer a case of polio or infantile paralysis as it was called in those days was confirmed in the village.  In fact the patient was a neighbour of ours.  She was only about eighteen. She attended the Orme School at Newcastle and was also a Sunday School teacher.  She was kept in an iron lung for a while to aid her recovery, but very sadly she died.  Fortunately there were no further outbreaks in the village and a few years after that children started receiving vaccines and medicines to prevent the disease, and consequently it became almost eradicated in this country.

Bagnall was a stimulating village to grow up in.  The young and old played cricket and rounders together.  We youngsters spent wonderful times sitting on the bales in the hay lofts at the farms.  We scrumped for apples at the hospital corner and even helped ourselves to eggs from under a chicken."

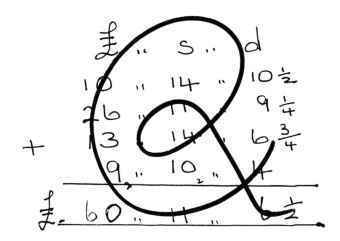

Mrs Billington had a distinctive way of marking the sums.

Mrs Stanistreet says goodbye in 1962.

Clewlow's Bank February 1940.

Light Oaks Reservoir (lost bus) February. 1940.

Clewlow's Bank by the church February. 1940.

Bagnall School 1947. Miss Shenton (Oakden) on the left, Mrs Edge and her daughter Annie. Mrs Billington (headmistress) and Miss Stanistreet on the right.

Back row L-R: June Eardley, Isobel Udall, Beryl Millington, Raymond Evans, Michael Glover, Peter Gibson, John Bowyer, Joe Dawson, Ronnie Astin, Anne Bainbridge.

2nd from the back: Miss Shenton (Oakden), Mrs Edge, Annie Edge, Peter Backett, Graham Astin, David Gibson, Arthur Mellor, John Woolley, Gary Baker, Helen Berrisford, Margaret Wallet, ?, John Mills, Mrs Billington (Headmistress) Jean Potts, Kathleen Beckett, Miss Stanistreet.

3rd: Margaret Corbishley, Irene Cork, Sheila Deaville, Ruth Cork, John Bailey, Christine Steele ? ? Malcolm Potts ? June Ball, Kay Holdcroft, Josephine Beckett, Margaret Sheldon ?

4th row: Dorothy Bailey, Gwen Gibson, Janet Mitchell ? Shenton ? Elaine Booth, Mary Warner, Sandra Glover ? June Steele, Graham Mills, Crosby.

Front row: Anne Newbrooks, Peter Cliff, George Gibson, Joyce Cliff, Wendy Hardacre, Monica Brereton ? ? John Eardley, John Philbin ? Alan Cork, Maureen Philbin.

Granny Hill's sweet shop and post office was in Rose Cottage (right side of photograph).

The old well at The Springs

The post office and shop opposite the Butter Cross (established in the 1940s and closed about 2000).

# Chapter 8
# Growing up in the Village

50 years ago village life was tranquil and slow compared to the present day. During the war years and in the early 1950s very few people owned cars, so travel was restricted. Fortunately there was a bus service - Milton Bus ran an excellent bus every hour from Hanley to Bagnall. The mustard yellow buses were very distinctive and their drivers and conductors were always courteous and helpful. One conductor in particular was a favourite with the children, he always called you 'Blossom' as he helped them up and down the steps.

Once a week, on a Wednesday, the bus company organised a market bus. It started in Hanley and ran to Bagnall, then on to Stanley and through Endon to Leek. The villagers would return with their baskets and bags full of fresh produce from the stalls.

Freda Ball recalls that on sunny days during the Summer months people from the Potteries came to the village as though it was some exotic holiday destination. They were usually loaded with picnics, rugs to sit on and other such paraphernalia. Some remained in the centre of the village, playing games and enjoying the fresh air. Others ventured down the steep hill to the Springs where the stream crosses the road. They paddled in the cool water or visited the old lichen-covered well. Some made their way to the Old Mills to climb over the rocks and explore the wooded areas.

Two of the ladies from the village, Mrs Goodall and Mrs Fisherwick, lived in the cottages on Springs Bank. They used to put out trestle tables full of sandwiches, cakes and drinks to sell. The visitors enjoyed their picnics and wearily climbed the hillside back to the bus stop to catch the bus home. The queues were sometimes quite long, with many eager faces hoping to find a place on the return bus journey.

In this period the local shop was an essential part of village life. When Madge Garrett moved to Bagnall in 1939, Granny Hill kept the sweet shop and post office in School Road. During the 1940s this shop closed and the combined shop and post office opposite the butter cross opened. The new shop sold groceries and vegetables, and was run very efficiently by Mrs Brassington. With some people, instead of paying for their purchases, Mrs Brassington made a note in her book and the customers paid later. At one time there appears to have been a café attached to the shop - the Rene Café, Bagnall appeared on the bus timetables.

Purchases from the village shop were augmented by two or three delivery vans that called on the householders each week. Some carried bread, others were loaded with meat and groceries. Coal wagons, piled high with black bags, were also regular visitors. There was no gas in the village and families would huddle around coal fires to keep warm during the winter.

After the war families started to venture to favourite holiday destinations again. Blackpool and holiday towns on the North Wales coast were places to visit, and could be reached fairly easily by train from Stoke station. Food rationing continued for some time after the war and families had to take their ration books on holiday with them. Sometimes they took their food supplies with them for their landladies to cook. Madge Garrett remembers her aunt and uncle travelling to camp in North Wales on a tandem, carrying their saucepans with them. One year they invited Madge and the family to join them. They thoroughly enjoyed the holiday, even though the wind blew their tent away.

Most householders had septic tanks in their gardens. These overflowed from time to time with their distinctive odour. Some people still had privies in their gardens and the sewage wagons made regular calls to empty them. The main sewage system did not reach the village until the 1950s. The sewage pipes came from the Milton area, up Bagnall Bank and through Light Oaks. The road was closed for several weeks to allow a passage to be blasted through the rocks.

Children living in the village had a great deal of freedom to explore and would often go off cycling or picnicking unaccompanied by adults. Rudyard, Leek, Milton, Hanley and Trentham were usually the parameters. Children had to leave the village for music lessons, tap and ballet lessons and to attend various secondary schools. Then there were visits to the cinemas or sometimes a visit to the Theatre Royal in Hanley.

Wireless sets played an important role in the villagers' lives. As well as the news programmes the adults enjoyed tuning in to listen to 'Much Binding in the Marsh', 'In Town To-night', 'Workers Playtime' and 'ITMA'. The youngsters enjoyed 'Childrens Hour' and 'Dick Barton, Special Agent'. After the war years television sets were gradually acquired. When Elizabeth II was crowned at Westminster Abbey in June 1953, people followed the spectacle on their own sets or those of their neighbours. The first screens were very small and the pictures were in black and white with just one channel. There were frequent breakdowns and the time then was filled with something like a picture of the potter turning his wheel. Coloured television did not arrive until the 1960s.

During the 1940s P.C. Hughes was the local policeman who dealt with law and order in the Bagnall/Light Oaks area. He lived in the police house on Clewlows Bank. He was a familiar sight on his bicycle and adults and children alike would stop to have a word with him. In 1948 P.C. Rushton took over from Bobby Hughes. He moved from Leek with his wife and two children Josephine and John. Josephine continued to attend school at Leek and although she was only 10 she walked from Bagnall to Stockton Brook each day. Sometimes she went down Clewlows Bank and then down Stanley Road to Stockton Brook station to catch the Leek bus. Sometimes she took the path through the Houghwood. John enrolled at Bagnall school where he remembers the children enjoyed helping to care for the pigs and chickens they kept in the garden. They always felt that as the local police constable's children, they had to behave themselves.

At this time notices were posted about vicious looking beetles called Colorado. These avaricious creatures were capable of causing a lot of damage to the potato crops and there was a reward of £5 to anyone who reported finding them. Some of the Bagnall school children found black and yellow beetles in one of the gardens and they calculated that if they received £5 for each beetle they would be able to purchase new bikes.  They collected them in a jam jar and took them to P.C. Rushton, who said he would inform them of any developments.  After two or three weeks he contacted them to inform them that the beetles had turned into ladybirds.

Josephine Sheldon (Rushton):

"My father was posted to Bagnall in 1948 as the village policeman.  His area stretched from the Rose and Crown at Stockton Brook, through Stanley and Bagnall, taking in Tomkin, Light Oaks, Kerry Hill and down to Milton.  He undertook his rounds each day by bicycle. I continued to attend my school in Leek and then a year later I transferred to Westwood Hall Girls' High School at Leek.

When I walked through the Houghwood to Stockton Brook I passed a café almost hidden in a secluded spot under the brow of the hill which had 'café' written on the roof.  It was situated in a very isolated spot and it was difficult to see where the customers came from.  In the springtime, it was surrounded  by daffodils which had been planted to spell out the name Houghwood.

We spent hours cycling around the village and exploring the countryside.  Sometimes we rode the pony that grazed down in the wood and at other times we played a rough type of netball on the Horse Pound outside the Stafford Arms -we didn't have any nets, but we had great fun.

Recently I was talking to my friend and we were reminiscing about life in Bagnall years ago.  She remembered the terrible floods during the Summer of 1927.  She was at Bagnall School and at the end of the afternoon she and her friends were unable to get through the floods at the bottom of the Springs Bank.  They were attempting to reach their homes on the Thorney Edge Road.  Apparently the stream at Blue Bridge was also impassable.  The children retraced their path back to the village and attempted to get home down the Hospital Bank, but this was badly flooded at Salters Wells.  Fortunately Billy Clews came along with a farm horse and was able to rescue the group.  He carried them through the water on the back of the horse.  When my friend eventually arrived home, she was surprised to see her mother sweeping floods of water out of their house.  Apparently the water had entered through the back door, swept through the house and out the front door. It was really surprising because the farm was on very high ground and no one could understand where the water had come from."

John Sheldon.

"When I was a youngster I lived at Springs Cottage Farm, Bagnall, opposite to where Peter Jackson's nursery is now.  My family was fortunate enough to have an Austin 7 car when I was a lad and we also had a pony and trap.

In those days the mains water supply had not reached the farm, and all ours came from the well at The Springs.  We had to transport large10 gallon churns full of water back to the farm. We kept cows, pigs and chickens and water was needed for them as well as for our washing and cooking. I remember that sometimes during a winters evening we would fancy a cup of tea, and if we had run out of water we had to take a bucket and walk along the road and through the wood to fill it at the well. It was strange, but I recall that sometimes if there had been a blizzard, the water that we had just drawn from the well appeared to steam.

At bath times we had to take it in turns to use the tin bath in front of the fire, and that took quite a bit of filling. The Matthews family, across the road from us, succeeded in diverting the water from the stream to their farm and sometimes we obtained water from it. Farther down the stream that ran into Stanley Pool there was a water wheel and a pump. From there water was pumped up to The Grange at Tomkin. Sometimes if it flooded, the pump would fail and the pipes would become blocked up. There was no proper sewage system, so we had a privy near to the house and this drained into a septic tank.

I remember that on one or two occasions I was startled to see a number of men crawling around the edges of the fields near to the hedgerows. I thought it might have been a break out from a local prison or asylum. It was during the war years and I discovered that the men were in the Home Guard and were undertaking a spot of training.

Like the other farmers in the area my father had a shotgun and would sometimes shoot a rabbit to supplement our rations. I remember some of the local mothers walking to Stockton Brook pushing their babies in prams to collect bottles of orange juice and cod liver oil. Normally our grocery supplies and vegetables were delivered by the Co-op van once a week and the Embrey's van delivered bread two or three times a week. I recall one bad winter when the bread van wasn't able to come due to exceptionally heavy snowfalls, I walked to the Rose and Crown at the bottom of Clewlows Bank and collected 15 loaves of bread. The local farmers had to clear the snow themselves and get their milk churns to a collecting point where the three roads meet just above the Blue Bridge.

The postman would deliver the letters and parcels by bicycle each morning. He had quite a demanding round that included Stanley, Thorney Edge and Tomkin as well as Bagnall. During the afternoons he would call at the various post boxes to empty them.

There were some interesting people in the village. Mr and Mrs Goodall lived in the middle of the row of cottages on Springs Bank and Mrs Goodall was quite a character. She seemed to be very knowledgeable about medical matters and if anyone was ill they would send for her, or call on her at the cottage.

Mr Lord of Bagnall Hall was an interesting man. He ran a very successful farm and in his spare time he charged up accumulators in one of his out buildings. The accumulators were used to operate the wireless sets and when they ran down they needed to be re-charged. His workshop was full of sockets, wires and plugs ñ in fact an Aladdin's cave to a small boy!

One farmer in the village had a brother who farmed over at Ipstones. When he sold some of his animals to his brother he walked with the animals all the way to Ipstones. I'm not sure how long it took to get there.

Another well-known farmer who lived at The Grange as well as running a farm at Tomkin, walked to Bellington Colliery each day. He worked his shift and then returned home in the evening to finish off the farm work. Farmers helped each other with the hay making and the harvest, with the hedging and ditching and with the milking. They advised each other over veterinary matters and were a great support to each other."

John Bailey:

"Sometime in the 1950s I joined the choir at Bagnall Church. At one of the Sunday services when Miss Jury was playing the organ, we had a power cut and all the electricity went off. My father, who was a member of the D.C.C. and the Church treasurer suggested that I squeeze through the little door to the side of the organ case. At the back of the organ there is a tiny room with bellows to pump the organ. I was helped through the doorway into this strange little room. I noticed that youngsters from the past had inscribed the walls with their initials and brief messages. I discovered that if I did not pump fast enough the organ went out of tune and sounded dreadful. After a while I slowed down on purpose and of course the organ sounded really weird. My father realised what I had been doing and I was in terrible trouble when I returned home.

On another occasion my Uncle Reg, who was the Churchwarden, was worried about some birds that were nesting in the bell tower and causing problems. The only way up to the loft was by ladder and Uncle Reg placed some ladders by the wall and asked me to go up and have a look. I was amazed by the splendid views from the top. When it was time to descend, however, I started to suffer from vertigo, and felt that I was frozen to the roof. Uncle Reg did his best to cajole and persuade me, but I felt I couldn't move. Eventually he had to send two more men up the ladder to bring me down.

A few years later when I started playing the organ, I had to go to the Church late one night to collect some music. It was pitch dark and I was just going to put the key in the door lock when the door slowly opened on its own. My heart turned over as a black mysterious figure emerged. After the initial shock I realised that it was Eric Docksey, who was the organist at that time. He had been practising with only the chancel light on and when he had finished he had switched the light off and made his way to the door in the dark - it was just a coincidence that we met in the doorway. Eric was a farmer and quite a character because he always came to Church on his tractor. In fact, he seemed to go everywhere on it."

Towards the end of the 1950s Mrs Brazier, the curate's wife, formed a Guildry group for the teenage girls, which was led by Anne Bainbridge. They wore a uniform consisting of white blouses and navy skirts and berets. The youngsters enjoyed country dancing, P.E. and games. Rounders on The Green was a great favourite. They enjoyed picnics at the Old Mills, and worked for badges that were awarded for cookery, needlecrafts, orienteering, and first aid. Shortly afterwards a group for the younger girls was formed. This was known as The Greenwood and was led by Mrs Audrey Haywood. All the girls attended a morning service once a month at St Chad's.

The Old Police House on Clewlow's Bank.

The new Police House was built in the 1950s. It was sold in the 1960s and became a private residence.

The Old Mills at Bagnall in
1920 and after the floods in
1927 destroyed them.

Lawn Farm dates from about 1791. (Photo 2005)

Manor House Farm. (Photo 2005)

Old Hall Farm. (Photo 2005)

Bank Farm. (Photo 2005)

The Garden Fete procession leaving the grounds of Bagnall Hospital in 1955. Margaret Sheldon was the Rose Queen and P.C. Rushton can be seen with his bicycle to the right of the photograph.

The Old Mills to-day.

# Chapter 9
# New Beginnings
# Mr Gibbs

Mrs Billington resigned in 1950 and in November of that year Mr Doug Gibbs was appointed headteacher. Mr Gibbs had been teaching at Cellarhead County Secondary Modern School. He had trained at St. Peter's Training College, Saltley and Loughborough College.

With Doug Gibbs' appointment, the school was filled with new life, new ideas and there was a tremendous enthusiasm for progress. A new relationship between the school and local parents was fostered by the formation of a Parents' Association. Drama groups for children and adults were established and Doug Gibbs was instrumental in forming the Bagnall Cricket Club.

In 1951 a new piano was presented to the school, together with a new gramophone and percussion instruments.

In July 1952 the Parents' association agreed to provide a suitable stage for the school.

Mr Gibbs' report to the Governors  September 1951.

*'Work in school was closely allied to the local Festival of Britain celebrations. At the end of June the school co-operated with other schools in the area in mounting a 'Festival Week' at Endon Secondary Modern School. On Saturday July 28th the school provided the basis of the Bagnall celebration in co-operation with the Parents' Association. Starting at 3pm a programme of athletics, sports, country dancing, national songs and open air plays lasted until 8pm. The occasion created great enthusiasm and the children acquitted themselves with great credit. Miss Stanistreet was responsible for the costumes and worked with great zeal and enthusiasm to ensure the success of the ventures.'*

Daphne Evans

"Mr Gibbs' time at Bagnall was happy and memorable. I thoroughly enjoyed the music and we used to listen to a programme on the radio called 'Singing together' with Barry Appleby, and also a programme called 'Rhythm and Melody' which taught us the rudiments of music. I enjoyed the art work and remember a huge frieze that we had made stretching along the walls of the classroom.

Janet Bainbridge, Kay Holdcroft and I pretended we were three of the characters out of one of our favourite comics 'School Friend'. We had a base down the Hough Wood in a holly bush of all places, and we made hoods and capes to wear. Mr Gibbs knew of our escapades and teased us sometimes.

I wrote an essay for Mr Gibbs entitled 'When Princess Elizabeth became heir presumptive'. I finished it off by writing 'God bless Elizabeth' and Mr Gibbs had written underneath, 'God bless Daphne'.

We had visits from the doctor who weighed and measured us, the nit nurse in her dark blue uniform, who combed through our hair searching for pests, and the dentist who checked our teeth, so we were well cared for. There was also the attendance officer known as the School Board Man. Many children who had been kept at home due to illness worried about the School Board Man coming to visit. Perhaps they expected him to drag them into school screaming and kicking.

Mr Gibbs passion was drama, music, country dancing and sports as well as being an excellent teacher in other academic subjects. He passed on this enthusiasm not just to the children in his care but their parents too. Having obtained a stage he formed a concert group called the 'Bagnallian Revels'. There was a singing group called 'The Corn Buskers', and my father wrote the words for the songs. Joe Wain played the guitar. They would sing verses about village life to the tune of 'Much Binding in the Marsh'. He encouraged my mother who was very shy to sing at the concerts and I remember her dressing up in trousers and carrying a stepladder as she sang, 'When I'm cleaning windows'. Mr Gibbs dressed up in a tutu and ballet shoes and sang, 'Nobody loves a fairy when she's forty'. Mr Townsend recited the monologue 'The green eye of the little yellow god'. Mr Gibbs also acted out a sketch about a surgeon performing an operation, but he did it behind a curtain so that only the shadows could be see as he extracted various strange objects from the patient's body. We all had tremendous fun.

I often had to narrate the plays because I found it difficult to remember the words. However I have vivid recollections of a nativity play where I played the part of a shepherd boy. I had had a nasty nose bleed earlier in the day and I wasn't feeling too well. I was waiting to go on the stage and I must have been day dreaming. The next thing I remembered was Miss Stanistreet giving me a huge push and I fell through the curtains. I can still feel that push now!

When we celebrated the Festival of Britain in 1951 Mr Gibbs had our stage taken up to the Horse Pound (now the Stafford Arms car park). We celebrated the festival with a performance of the play 'The Sleeping Beauty' and we had sports and country dancing. We performed dances like Brighton Camp, The Durham Reel, If All The World Were Paper, Gathering Peaspods, Black Nap, Rufty Tufty and the Ribbon Dance, but sadly no maypole dancing. After a wonderful day, it was time to dismantle the stage and return it to its storage place under the bike shed.

There was one unhappy incident that I remember. It was after we had taken our 11+ exams and I had passed to go to the grammar school. Some of the children suddenly seemed to turn against me. One day whilst I was in the cloakroom they circled around me teasing and being generally spiteful to me. I was extremely upset and as this sort of behaviour continued for a while I became quite sick. I reached the stage where I did not want to go to school. However, my father must have had a word with Mr Gibbs because quite suddenly it all stopped.

In those days the school really was the centre of village life. Life revolved around the school, not the church. The school bells signalled the passing of the day. The village life revolved around the school year and influenced everything that seemed to happen in the area. It was the village meeting place, the place for entertainment as well as academic achievements, even our medical centre to a point, our advice centre and at one stage, our library."

The minutes of the managers' meetings record what was going on in the school with changing attitudes to pupils and the improvement to the fabric of the school.

On the 7 July 1952 a minute recorded the managers' appreciation of the headteacher's enthusiasm for the welfare of the school. The headteacher in turn expressed his hope that a uniform would be adopted for all pupils. Another minute from the July meeting showed that a tender for the conversion of the 'out offices' to water closets by Messrs Yardley and Whittaker had been accepted, subject to the approval of the Ministry of Works. (After nearly eighty years, the Victorian lavatories were to be replaced). The managers at this time included: Major T. Harvey, Mr W. Baddeley, Mr G. Chawner and Mr J.W. Grindon. In the Autumn they were joined by Mr E. Brown and Mr W. Ball.

At the September meeting concern was expressed concerning the need for fire fighting equipment. (A portent for what was to happen 17 years later). The state of the school garden at the rear of the school house was discussed and a request was made to the County Garden Staff for assistance.

In January 1953 the Physical Education Organiser had visited the school and was concerned about the lack of space around the school building for games and physical activities. A suggestion was made that enquiries should be made to find a suitable field close to the school to use as a playing field.

The school was having quite an impact on village life as it was pointed out that recent school activities had included a concert, a Christmas Party and a Flower Festival. It was about this time that it was agreed that the two honours boards in the Infants' classroom were an anachronism and it was agreed to take them down and possibly use them as notice boards in the schoolyard. By May 1953 resurfacing had taken place in the Girls' and Infants' playgrounds, a geyser had been installed in the staff toilet, and there had been some help in restoring the school garden. However there had been no success in finding a field suitable to use as a playing field and this was a great disappointment. Nevertheless new washbasins were being installed in the cloakrooms and a new form of hot water system was proposed.

In June 1953 the school celebrated Queen Elizabeth's coronation with various events. A sum of 1s 11d per child had been allocated to purchase something to commemorate the occasion. Mr Gibbs reported to the managers that he had decided that fish tanks would be appropriate.

By December 1953 there were problems with the staffing of the school as Miss Stanistreet had been absent with a severe illness and Mrs Stephenson had also been poorly. Therefore it was agreed by the managers that Mrs Cooper should be engaged to help out during this difficult time. Visitors to the school at this time were H.R. Taylor, Mr Scott, the P.E. organiser, and Miss Chester, the school meals organiser. They had all expressed satisfaction with the work of the school.

It was about this time that enquiries were made about the possibility of the headmaster moving into the schoolhouse, but it was already occupied by the caretaker.

## Jim Bailey (Grandson of Mary Jane Harvey)

"I wasn't very keen on the school dinners at that time, so I used to take a packed lunch from home. Usually I finished my sandwiches fairly quickly and would be the first out into the playground ready to play. One particular day I had finished lunch and was on my own in the playground, waiting for my friends to join me. In the adjoining field, which belonged to Reg Clowes, Mr Evans was at work turning the newly mown grass over. Amongst the grass he had found a large number of cigarette packets that we boys had made into aeroplanes to fly in competition with each other. Mr Evans decided to throw them all back into the school yard and I was the only boy there to pick them up. I was so popular with my pals when they eventually joined me, and we were able to do lots of flying with our new stock of aeroplanes!"

## Jan Crumpler (Bainbridge)

"Mr Gibbs was a great teacher liked by all. Kay Holdcroft, Daphne Evans and I had great fun with him. We called ourselves 'The Silent Three' and he played along with us. When Miss Stanistreet was away, Kay Holdcroft and I always took the Infants for the day and we loved it. Miss Stanistreet wasn't too well at that time and she seemed to be absent a lot.

I was in a play, Sleeping Beauty, which was performed at Endon School. I was the wicked fairy who turned into a good fairy. Kay was the Sleeping Beauty.

When we were teenagers I remember the dances we used to have in the two lower rooms. The partition was pushed back and we danced the night away. The youth club was very popular, and Joe Pratt and Edith Deaville taught us all types of dancing. Annie Edge, her sister and her mother produced the refreshments for us."

## Margaret Ball (Beckett)

"The school day would begin by usually running to catch the bus which would take me to Bagnall to begin school at 9am.

The school buildings were built of grey stone and consisted of three classrooms, each with their own separate entrances. There were also separate cloakrooms with large coat hooks. The classroom windows were high and I was unable to see outside. The two top classrooms were separated by a large, wooden folding partition.

Miss Stanistreet was my first teacher.  My first day I sat by Joyce Cliff and quickly learned that too much talking would result in either having to sit with hands on heads or having our knuckles rapped with a ruler.  Miss Stanistreet always seemed to be a very old lady, who had very long hair.  She once told us that she could actually sit on her hair it was that long.  She did however wear it clipped up somehow.  She played the piano and we said prayers with our hands together and eyes closed   At the end of each day we would sing:

> *Thank you for the world so sweet,*
> *Thank you for the food we eat,*
> *Thank you for the birds that sing,*
> *Thank you God for everything.  Amen.*

Miss Shenton (Mrs Oakden following marriage) was far from my favourite teacher.  As well as sums and writing,  each day we did knitting and sewing, neither of which I could do.  No allowances were made for the fact that I was left handed and therefore sewed differently to everyone else.  If possible in this lesson I would opt for cork-wool.

Mr Gibbs had the school bell located in this classroom, high up in the ceiling with a long rope attached.  It was rung every morning until everyone had arrived and again during the day (dinner time and play times).  It was considered a great privilege if you were chosen to toll the bell.  There was also a small board in the classroom, which was filled in every day:

    Nos. on roll
    Nos. absent
    Nos. in school

At playtimes we used three playgrounds, where everyone seemed to run about a lot. We played skipping and played. Everyone had to clear the first playground when there was a delivery of coke for the school boiler.

I have a particular memory of Mr Gibbs asking the class who could use the phone in a phone box.  I put up my hand (although I wasn't too sure if I could).   I was chosen to make a call everyday from the telephone box outside the Post Office to Baddeley Green School (as they supplied the dinners) to advise them of the number of dinners required. When the telephone was out of order on many occasions I had to go to Mrs Lord's house (Bagnall Hall) and she always left me an apple or banana on her hall chair to eat after I had finished the call.

I can't quite remember when school dinners were introduced, but I recall that the dinners were served by the caretaker, Mrs Edge and her daughter Annie. The best thing they served in my opinion was chocolate pudding.  This consisted of cardboard pastry smeared with chocolate paste, which always seemed to end up with an imprint of Mrs Edge's thumb in the chocolate paste.

Our school outing was a trip to New Brighton.  I remember that Florrie Gibson from the shop at Light Oaks let me have 2ozs of sherbet lemons to take on the trip.  I don't know which I was more excited about - the trip or the sherbet lemons.

On the day that George VI died we were all ushered into Miss Stanistreet's class to listen to the announcement on the radio that the King was dead, and Mr Gibbs was constantly tolling the bell.

Sadly in 1954 Mr Gibbs tendered his resignation, to take effect from the end of August that year, so the managers and education officials had to concentrate on the appointment of a new headteacher. One candidate who had been asked to consider the post, wrote to H.R. Taylor at the County Education Offices expressing her views about the school. She was clearly not impressed:

*'Curiosity however, took me to Bagnall, and I feel dismayed and discouraged that you should rate my ability and my ambition so low to think that I should be interested in, and apply for, a school like that.*

*There are many reasons why neither the school nor the village impressed me. You said the fabric was in good condition, but perhaps you have not seen the school for some time. Although it is no concern of mine I think I ought to mention to you that the posts of one of the gates is unsafe and liable to fall off on anyone who attempts to open it.'*

Bagnall Cricket Club. Keith Boughey and Roy Holland are the umpires.
Joe Wain is in the centre of the front row, with Doug Gibbs on the far right.

Bagnall C.C. Dr. Hallam from Clewlow's Bank is in the dark suit with Ken Evans just behind him.  Doug Gibbs (Headmaster), Roy Kilfoil, Joe Wain and Jim Boughey are some of the members in the middle row. Patrick Handley is to the right of the front row with Peter Gibbs, who played for Derbyshire, next to him.

Bagnall Cricket Club.  Front L-R: Peter Handley, Ken Evans, Peter Gibbs, Roy Kilfoil.
2nd row: includes David Gibson, Mr Handley, Mr Boughey, Joe Wain & Doug Gibbs
3rd row: includes Gordon Simpson, Keith Boughey, Bill Brassington, Fred Potts and Arthur Roberts.
4th row: includes John Brindley and Alan Tellwright.

Bagnall Cricket Club wives.
Front: Winnie Axon, Ann Gibbs, Molly Townsend, Mrs Boughey, Mrs Handley.
Middle: Rosemary Gibbs, Gerty Jones, Nelly Pickering.  Back: Mrs Davis, Dorothy Boughey, Mrs Garibaldi.

Festival of Britain celebrations at Endon School.  Bagnall School children performed The Sleeping Beauty.
L to R: Gwen Gibson, Margaret Beckett, Janet Bainbridge, Audrey Beardmore, Miss Stanistreet, Joyce
Corbishley, Mrs Oakden, Daphne Evans, Jean Bowyer.

Festival of Britain Committee 1951. Front L to R: Lily Evans, Mary Wain, Sybil Woolley, Doug Gibbs, Dorothy Holdcroft, Effie Stanistreet, Pat Brammer, Enid Key.
Back: ? Jim Townsend, Percy Bailey, Roy Holland, Bernard Evans, Fred Potts, Guy Gibson, Mr Bott.

Bagnall Coronation Party June 1953. The working party of ladies from the Church and the W.I.
Back: Rosie Roberts, Mary Wain, Ann Bott, Mrs Brayford, Mrs Glover, Mrs Sheldon, Mrs Sutton, Mrs Holdcroft
Front: includes Mrs Bowen, Mrs Evans, Annie Edge, Mrs Haywood.

Bagnall Festival of Britain celebrations. 1951

The cast of The Sleeping Beauty.

Back L-R: Maureen Bott, Audrey Beardmore, Joyce Corbishley, Jean Bowyer, Gwen Gibson, Graham Astin,
Margaret Beckett, Tony Bloor, Daphne Evans,John Salmon, Elaine Booth, Tony Bott, Monica Brereton, Wendy Hardacre.
Middle L-R: John Bailey, John Woolley, Philip Handley, Linda Challinor, Mr Gibbs, Kay Holdcroft, Malcolm Potts, Janet Bainbridge, Patrick Handley, Maureen Ball.
Front L-R: Louise Whitfield, Ruth Cork, John Townsend, John Rushton, George Gibson, Pat Hopkins, Margaret Mellor,
Margaret Sheldon, Peter Beckett, Janet Mitchell, Christine Steele, Helen Berrisford.

The last Christmas Party at the school.  Mr. Ballington (Headmaster) and Mrs Betty Hughes are at the back.

The Last Christmas Party at Bagnall School in 1968.
Mrs M. Johnson is helping to hand out the sandwiches.

# Chapter 10
# The Last Years

Mr F. Ballington from Hatton in Derbyshire was appointed as the new headteacher in September 1954 and he set about improving the school with enthusiasm.

In May 1955 the managers agreed to purchase the field next to the school on Clewlow's Bank to be used as a playing field. The Education Committee was left to negotiate the purchase of the site. At last there would be more space for pupils to play football games, and enjoy sports events.

In 1956 the caretaker, Mrs Edge died. She had dedicated many years of her life to the school and now a successor had to be appointed. Three people applied for the post. Mrs Edge had occupied the school house for a good many years, and the chairman of the managers was asked by the Education Committee whether the headmaster might like to occupy the house in place of a new caretaker. The chairman reminded the managers that the schoolhouse was originally provided for the headteacher and that until Mr Hargreaves time successive headteachers had lived there. The chairman recommended that the house should revert back to that type of accommodation.

It was also resolved that the clerk should write to the Ministry of Labour and to the National Service local office at Leek to see whether there were any suitable disabled persons who might like to be considered for the position of part-time caretaker

The following month Annie, Mrs Edge's daughter, was appointed as the new caretaker, but the managers informed her that no home would be provided with the post. She agreed to accept the terms, although she had lived in the schoolhouse for many years. The managers now realised that the caretaker was now without living accommodation, and they hoped to help to provide alternative accommodation, possibly at the old police house half way down Clewlow's bank.

Mr. Ballington's workload was heavy as he had to run the school and teach his class full time without the help of any secretarial assistance, so in May 1957 he requested that a secretary should be appointed on a part-time basis. Mrs K. Gosling was appointed and was greatly appreciated.

The question of appointing a deputy head was raised at one of the manager's meetings, but as the school was classified only as a group one school it was not considered necessary. By this time one or two assistants were employed to help supervise the children at dinner times.

The following year the underdrawing of the old Victorian lavatories was done and work had begun on the sewage plant. By September of that year the playing field had been purchased and surveyed for fencing. A deputation from the County Council had visited the head teacher's house had a number of repairs were agreed on.

In September 1958 the numbers on the roll were:

| | | |
|---|---|---|
| Class J2 | pupils 35 | teacher  Mr. Ballington |
| Class J1 | pupils 25 | teacher  Mrs J.E. Cooper |
| Infants | pupils 25 | teacher   Miss E Stanistreet |

40 children received school meals, for which they paid, and only 1 child qualified for free meals.  12 children ate sandwiches for lunch daily and 55 children drank a bottle of milk each day.

In November 1958 there were changes to the supervisory staff.  Mrs G. Pratt, Senior general assistant ceased her employment and Mrs A. Haywood acted as the Senior general assistant with increased hours.  Mrs J. Holdcroft took on the duties of General Assistant at 5 hours a week in addition to her duties as Supervisory Assistant.  By this time the number of children on roll had dropped to 83.

In 1959 closer ties were being established with St. Chad's Church in the village, and some assemblies were conducted there with the support of Rev Kenneth Brazier.

As the building had been in use for 85 years as a school it is not surprising that the fabric was in need of some updating.  The managers drew the Education Authority's attention to the poor heating, and the really uncomfortable draughts in some of the classrooms.  The ventilation in the old air raid shelters needed attention, and the overall feelings amongst the managers was that the school buildings needed to be brought up to regulation standards.

After three years in her post as caretaker Miss Edge was finding it difficult to make three or four journeys each day to the school to stoke the boilers and tendered her resignation.

The numbers on the roll were still dropping and by September 1960 there were 74 children.  However the school was being fully utilised by the WI, the Youth Club, the Parents Association, the Parish Council and Bagnall Social Club.  The latter held  nine whist drives on Saturday evenings during the Autumn term.  During Mr Ballington's time the name of the school was changed from Bagnall County Primary School to Moorlands County Primary School, Bagnall.

After 42 years as the Infants' teacher at Bagnall School, Miss Stanistreet decided it was time for a change and tendered her resignation, to take effect from the end of the Summer Term 1962.  On 16th July 1962 a presentation evening was held to commemorate her retirement.  Major T. Harvey, chairman of the managers, presided over the occasion and presented to the school an oak lectern, suitably inscribed to commemorate Miss Stanistreet's long and valued service.  The headmaster presented Miss Stanistreet with a tea service, a kettle and a cheque.  Mr G. Pickford, chairman of the Parent Teacher Association presented her with a cut glass rose bowl on behalf of the association.  Then Mr D.K. Gibbs, headteacher from 1951 to 1954 gave a tribute to Miss Stanistreet. Following the presentation, pupils past and present, with the assistance of Miss Teresa Wain and Mrs B. Hughes, gave a music concert under the direction of Mr Ballington.  It must have been a day to remember!

Mrs Betty Hughes took over Miss Stanistreet's post as the Infant's teacher. She also took over the care of Miss Stanistreet's cat which lived at the school. The cat, Totty, spent its days curled up on a cushion on Miss Stanistreet's high backed Windsor chair, much to the delight of the children. Mr Ballington was not too endeared to Totty as it frequently left paw prints over the roof of his car.

During the Autumn term the school settled into the normal routine, but the Winter months brought really bad weather and a number of children were absent, especially on the days that the bus from Milton did not arrive. The taxi was unable to collect the children from Stanley from Jan 21st until February 10th. The attendance was also adversely affected by 53 cases of chicken pox breaking out.

On October 4th 1963 Mr Ballington reported that he had noticed a blaze in the boiler house. Some wood used for kindling had caught fire in one of the corners. Leek fire brigade was called whilst Mr Godman, tackled the blaze with two fire extinguishers. The only damage sustained was to two yards of electrical conduit. The blaze was probably caused by the flue door not closing properly.

During the winter of 1963 there were problems with the flush toilets being frozen up. A water wagon visited the school to supply water, but the conditions were so bad for the children that Mr Godman wrote to the Staffordshire Education Committee to complain. Even though the toilets had been converted to flush toilets, the boys' urinals were still outside in the open.

In 1965 Mrs K. Gosling resigned as Secretary at the school, and Mrs M. Hilditch was appointed to the post for 9 hours a week.

On January 10th 1965 Mr Howells visited the school to discuss the possibility of a youth service hut being built, together with a new canteen, staff room and toilets. However he came to the conclusion that as the windows needed renewing it might be easier to build a new school on the playing fields.

Denise Johnson

"I started Bagnall School after Easter 1963, which was the term of my fifth birthday. My mother used to help me with my reading and writing at home. When I was six, having caught the measles, I spent three weeks at home. My mother was working part time, so my gran came to look after me, and taught me all my tables up to the 12xs table. I still remember them to-day. We were in the first class until we were seven, and my teacher was Mrs Betty Hughes.

When I went into another class I was put into Mrs Sergeant's. She was a very nice teacher, but my mother wasn't happy because she thought I was in the wrong class, so she complained to Mr Ballington and I was put into Mrs Wood's class. I cannot remember much about the lessons, but I learned Fractions, Geography, History and English. Two afternoons a week we had craft lessons. I embroidered some aprons, knitted some soft toys, and embroidered a handkerchief case. After two years in Mrs Wood's class I moved up into the top class, but we returned to Mrs Wood for two afternoons a week for craft. I did mot have art lessons very often.

Mr Ballington, the headmaster, used to live in the schoolhouse. His garden was situated between the playground and the school field and it looked lovely with roses and other flowers. He kept several hives of bees and early in the Autumn we were allowed to buy the honey. It was delicious coming fresh from the hives.

Coming up to Christmas 1967 foot and mouth disease hit the farms in Bagnall. Manor House Farm was one of the farmers affected and his field joined the schoolyard. The stone wall was low enough to see over, so a lot of us stood watching at break times and dinner times, as the dead cows were laid one on top of another in a pit in the ground and lime was spread over them."

In November 1967 foot and mouth disease spread rapidly throughout the British Isles. Staffordshire was declared a controlled area on 1st November, although at that time there were no cases in the county, the nearest cases being in Cheshire. The headlines in the Sentinel on November 4th read, 'Staffs Fight to Stem Farm Disaster', as the first case in the county at Gnosall was confirmed.

The cattle had to be slaughtered even at the farms where the animals were healthy, so all the farms surrounding the village were affected in one way or another. People arrived from the Ministry of Agriculture and sealed off the farms, forbidding any visitors and isolating the residents. The children living at the farms were not allowed to return after school and they had to stay with friends or relations whilst everywhere was disinfected.

Bagnall was hit harder than anywhere else in the north of the county. On 22nd November foot and mouth at Manor Farm was confirmed and 91 beasts had to be slaughtered. On the 25th at Bank House Farm 75 cattle had to be destroyed. The two farms within a very small community.

The plea in the Sentinel on November 28th read, 'The County needs to be Reassured that all Possible Steps are being Taken to Contain the Epidemic'. Complaints were made that golf was still being played on the golf course only a few feet away from Manor House Farm. Children attending Bagnall School had to keep to the roads and not use the short cuts across the fields.

By the end of the month 200,000 animals had been slaughtered countrywide. Mrs Margaret Whalley lived on a farm at Stanley at time and she recalls that the farmers who had animals in fields near to the infected farms also had to have their herds and flocks slaughtered. Fortunately their farm had a road around their land boundaries, but they were warned to take all their cattle indoors and to keep them there for as long as the epidemic lasted. They had a lorry to transport some young calves to the cowsheds so that they wouldn't have to walk on the roadways.

In 1965 Mrs Millie Hilditch returned to the school she had attended as a child in her new capacity as the school secretary and was employed for two afternoons a week. Kath

Gosling had retired earlier that year. Kath had her desk in the back corner of Mr Ballington's classroom near the partition, but Millie had a desk in a corner of Mrs Hughes' room near to the window that looked into Mr Ballington's room. A screen was placed around the desk, but she felt sure she must have disturbed Mrs Hughes with her typing, although she never complained. Millie's duties included dealing with the correspondence, typing out reports and filling in forms.

During the Autumn of 1968 proposals were made to draw up plans to connect the school to the main sewage system, and new toilets were requested. The school obviously still needed quite a lot of work doing to it to bring it up to standard. In January 1969 requests were made again for a staff room. The original request had been made four years earlier, but nothing had been forthcoming. There is a lovely anecdote at this time in a communication to the headmaster.

*'The Chief Constable regretted that because of heavy duty commitments it would not be possible to provide a course on horse riding. He would however, be happy for a mounted Branch officer to visit the school from time to time to give talks on road safety.'*

On Friday 14th March 1969 people working inside the classrooms felt that the rooms were uncomfortably hot and they were forced to open the windows for some fresh air.

They could not have foreseen what would happen the following day. On the Saturday Mr Bernard Vickers, a school manager, was passing the school at about 8.25pm when he noticed that the school building was on fire. He called the fire brigade and they arrived at 8.55pm. However due to a strong wind and very low water pressure in the mains nothing could be done to prevent its utter destruction. Mr Ballington had been away that weekend and hurried back as soon as he heard the news.

Denise Johnson:

"On March 15th 1969 something happened to the school boiler which was situated under the middle and top class in the school and there was a major fire which gutted the school. There was only the stone shell left standing, and as this was unsafe, the school was pulled down. Other pupils might tell you how they felt, but for me it was a double blow as I was still recovering from the death of my father.

After the half term holiday we went by bus to Werrington School in Salter's Lane. My classroom was a mobile where all the juniors were together. The Infants were in a separate part. Some of the children who were at school with me were, Robert Gibson, Suzanne Legan, Alan Platt, John Dunnett, the son of the vicar at Bentilee, Jane Greatbach, Paul Hughes, the son of Betty Hughes, Stephen Edge, Mark Thursfield, Simon Thursfield, David Pearson, Paul Seddon, the son of Doctor Seddon, Caroline Gosling, Lynn Hughes and Ian Millington, Julie Podmore, Dorothy Philip, the daughter of the vicar of Abbey Hulton, and Elizabeth and Sarah Mankey, the daughters of the vicar of Bagnall."

Betty Hughes (Allmark):

"I came to Bagnall to teach in September 1962. I was responsible for teaching the rising 5 to 7 year olds. This was quite a challenge having such an age range in one class, but I looked forward to the challenge and soon had the class organised.

My years spent teaching at Bagnall were extremely happy. At first there were only three classes, myself as the Infants teacher, Mr Godman as the 7-9 teacher and the headmaster Mr Ballington, for the 9-11 year olds.

What a happy school it was. I can't remember any of the 5 year olds being upset at all. The older children took them under their wing and looked after them.

I have many happy memories, among them the Christmas concerts we held each year. The whole school took part in the concert so no child was left out. I spent hours making costumes before the event, often burning the midnight oil, but I was well rewarded when I saw the children performing.

The Christmas parties were really something. The staff shopped for presents for the children and each child was treated as an individual. They each received a present which we knew they would appreciate. The parties went on all day with films, games, and a wonderful tea provided by the Parent Teacher Association.

Another happy memory is the sports day held towards the end of the Summer term each year. It was always held on a Saturday so that fathers as well as mothers could come to cheer on their off spring. A great time was had by all, everyone trying their best to win. Rather amusing to see the little ones who were competing for the first time. They didn't care to be seen as the first so they waited for another child to 'catch up' with them, It all added to the fun. Help was given by the PTA and the staff were most grateful.

Lessons at Bagnall School were most enjoyable. It was before the National Curriculum was brought into action and the children were allowed to develop at their own pace. We had long nature walks to the Springs, the Old Mills and Stanley Pool. Interesting lessons would develop from these walks, with a little imagination we could incorporate subjects such as maths, geography and history, all playing a vital part in the childrens' development.

The school had a good reputation and pupils outside the area wanted to attend so we had to employ more teachers. Mrs June Warwood was the first and she took the 7 year olds, and then Morag Jones came to take the 7-9 year olds.

The school continued to thrive until tragedy struck. It was a Saturday night and there was a very high wind. The school caught fire and everything in the building was lost. We lost all our records and everyone including the children was devastated. We had a two day closure and were sent to Werrington, Salters Lane, where we shared the school with the Werrington children. The caretaker there was an old pupil of Bagnall School and she made us really welcome.

We had several episodes travelling to Werrington. Sometimes the bus wouldn't show up and I had to telephone to see where it was. Another time we had an erratic driver who landed us in the ditch and we had to climb out through the emergency door.

Sometimes the children didn't mix too well and they were unkind to each other. Altogether it was not a happy time for any of us, and we didn't know what would happen to us at the end of the term. Eventually we found out that a new school was being built at Endon because St. Luke's was full to overflowing, and we were told that we would be moving down to Endon. Great excitement, but how were we going to travel? Endon High School already had a bus, but they couldn't accommodate all our pupils. However an extra bus was put on, and the bus still takes pupils to this day.

We moved to Endon in September 1969 and, yes, we had the same children and staff, but it wasn't quite like Bagnall. At Bagnall we had the open countryside around us, but at Endon we were on the edge of a large housing estate. You could only take the rising 5 year olds from Endon because we had filled the school. Our good reputation followed us and before long we needed extra classrooms. Many of our pupils went on to higher education and university, and now have good secure jobs. It was a privilege to teach these children and I treasure my memories."

On Monday, 17th March, the Assistant Director of Education, Mr Copley, Mr Price (County Inspector), Mr Gask (County Architect) and Mr. Smith (head of Supplies Dept) visited Mr Ballington at the school house to discuss the future of the school.

It was agreed that after two days closure the 89 children would be taken by bus each day to Saltway Primary School, Werrington, where they would be accommodated in two prefabricated huts. The head and staff were to report to Saltway Primary on Monday 18th to receive some furniture and prepare the rooms for the arrival of the children.

Mr Fletcher, the Chief County Inspector, visited to offer advice and to comfort the staff, as they had been badly shaken by the event. The head at Saltway, Mr Chalmers, and his staff, were very cooperative as they helped their unexpected visitors to settle into their new classrooms. Two buses conveyed the children to Werrington each day. However both the pupils and teachers were surprised to see that as they caught the buses on the first day to travel to Werrington the old school buildings were already being demolished. At Saltway two infants classes occupied one hut and the two junior classes occupied the other.

Mr G. Price was there to welcome them on the first day and agreed to appoint Miss Helen Hughes as a temporary part time teacher to help with the situation. Mrs M. Hilditch, the school clerical assistant increased her workload and was employed for four days a week The kitchen staff agreed to resume their normal duties and were transported to Werrington by Mrs A. Haywood. By April 2nd the children had been reorganised as follows:

| Class 1 | 5-7 years | 32 children | Mrs B. Hughes |
| Class 2 | 7-9 years | 27 children | Mrs J. Warwood |
| Class 3 | 9-11 years | 30 children | Mrs M. McGillivray |

Mr Ballington helped by teaching classes and groups. However things must have been difficult because by the end of term all the kitchen staff resigned.

Millie Hilditch (Fowler):

"On the night of the fire I was looking out of my kitchen window, and I could see the flames leaping from the roof of the school building. We phoned the fire brigade and we went round to see if anything could be done. There was nothing we felt able to do and as I couldn't bear to watch, I returned home. Later I was able to see where my desk had been and to recognise the burnt out frame of my typewriter.

The following Wednesday we all took the bus to Saltway School at Werrington. There were some vacant classrooms there, as some of the pupils had moved to the new school that had just been built. The caretaker had attended Bagnall school as a child and she was really kind to us. It was really cold in the huts and she would stoke up the stoves for us to keep us warm. I worked for four days a week instead of two afternoons, based in the headmaster's room. I had to re-order everything and collect together all the information about the children, to replace the records lost in the fire.

After the Summer holidays we were transferred to Endon Hall School where I worked in the staff room. It was very different to being at the school at Bagnall, but gradually we settled in."

At a special meeting held a the headmaster's house at the end of March that year, it was hoped that the school could be rehoused in mobiles on the school playing field, but eventually the problem was resolved when the authorities decided that the children from Bagnall could move to the new school that had recently been completed at Endon. All the staff had to reapply for their jobs and when term closed on 22nd July 1969 the school equipment was moved from Werrington to Endon.

The final closure notices for the Moorland Primary School, Bagnall, were posted in November of that year. Of course this also meant the end of the youth club. After almost 100 years serving the community, Bagnall Primary school and all that it meant and stood for had come to an end, but the memories that passed through the minds of the villagers watching the fire that tragic night will live on.

The fire only spared the schoolhouse, which some years later received a new lease of life when it was extended over the school garden to form the new Moorland Village Hall. The old air raid shelters are buried somewhere underneath, and the covered shed which ran from the school to the garden has been replaced by the toilet block. The car park now covers the area where the old school stood, and the school field has become the village playing field. In the past the school was a vital, vibrant part of the Village community and it is a tribute to the villagers that the area is still the centre of village life.

St Chad's choir and church members in the late 1950s.

Bagnall Bank at Light Oaks before it was widened

Bagnall Sunday School afloat, Sept 1955.  Standing on right: Stan Carter (Curate), Mr & Mrs Hemming.
Front: Mr Bill Haywood, Mrs Betty Sutton.
Centre, in barge, Bob Shufflebottom, Joyce Rowley, Marion Ford, Margaret Corbishley, Mrs Bott, Mrs Mountford, Mrs Clo
Other youngsters in the barge include Josephine Beckett, Elaine Booth, Monica Brereton, Jennifer Sutton, Mary Warne
Sandra Glover, Margaret Wallet, Jennifer Booth, Anne Bainbridge, Ann Dawson, Peter Hall, Maureen Bott.